The Childproofing Checklist

The Childproofing Checklist

A Parent's Guide to Accident Prevention

by Mary Metzger
and Cinthya P. Whittaker

Foreword by
Martin R. Eichelberger, M.D.

Doubleday
NEW YORK
1988

Information in appendix 1 and 2 provided courtesy of The National Capital Poison Center, Georgetown University Hospital, Washington, D.C.

Illustrations by Katrina Kelsch

Library of Congress Cataloging-in-Publication Data

Metzger, Mary.
    The childproofing checklist: a parent's guide to accident prevention/Mary Metzger & Cinthya P. Whittaker; foreword by Martin R. Eichelberger.
        p.   cm.
    Bibliography: p.
    ISBN 0-385-24263-8
    1. Safety education—United States. 2. Children's accidents—United States—Prevention. I. Whittaker, Cinthya P. II. Title.
HQ770.7.M48   1988
649'.1'0289—dc19   87-36415
                                                    CIP

O

This book is lovingly dedicated to
the safety of children everywhere

ACKNOWLEDGMENTS

With special thanks to our families . . .
> John, Eliot, and Ian Metzger
> Jim, Adam, and Lindsey Whittaker
> Joe, Margaret, Paul, Dick, Tom, and Joe Raftery
> Bob and Toni Pandini
> Bob and Gloria Whittaker
> Bob Metzger and Mary Pierce

To our friends for their support and
encouragement . . .
> Chester Aaron
> Robert Brotzman
> Carole Dempsey
> Carolyn Funk
> Andrew Haugh
> Diane Long
> and especially Jeff Long

And the others who made a difference . . .
> Gwen Edelman
> Ceil Hendrickson
> Beth and Tim Herrick, M.D.s
> Sheri Hoopes
> Katrina Kelsch
> David Maddox
> Amy Marasco
> Rose Ann Soloway
> and our editors Rachel Klayman and Anne
>   Sweeney

Contents

AUTHOR'S NOTE

Naturally, the information contained in this book applies to both sexes; but we found it awkward constantly to change from "he" to "she" and "his" to "hers." So for the sake of smooth reading and fairness, we alternate male and female pronouns chapter by chapter.

Foreword

Susan Anderson is a conscientious mother. By the time her son Mark was eleven months old, she had read many books on child rearing and child safety. She also bought a number of safety devices to keep Mark out of trouble. She was always on the lookout to protect him from injury, or so she thought.

One evening about six o'clock, while heating water to cook some pasta, the UPS truck arrived with a delivery. Moving quickly to answer the door, Susan left Mark, who was in his walker, in the kitchen by himself. After signing for her package and thanking the driver, Susan heard a scream. It was a cry she would hear over and over again in her sleep for months to come.

Mark had braced himself on the brim of his walker and reached up to see what Mommy was cooking in that shiny blue pot on the stove. The entire pot of boiling water spilled onto his face, neck, and right arm. Within seconds, the time between curiosity and exploration for a child, Mark had become another tragic statistic and an "accident" victim. Mark suffered third-degree burns and spent the rest of the year in and out of the hospital for treatment and evaluation.

Mark is one of the approximately twenty-two million children (one in four) involved in accidents annually. Thousands of these children sustain major injuries, suffer long-term disabilities, or are permanently disabled.

In this important book, Ms. Metzger and Ms. Whittaker demonstrate that most accidents don't "just happen," and that people are not helpless in preventing them. The authors introduce you to the concept of "childproofing" your home—that is, making your home a safe environment for your children. By outlining the potential hazards that exist in each room of a home, they show us the important role that we, as parents, play in the area of child safety.

It remains a widely unrecognized fact that accidental injuries are the leading killer of children in this country, claiming nearly 10,000 lives each year. A large majority of these childhood deaths could have been prevented if parents and caregivers had simply taken the time to check their children's environments for hazards. Objects that are safe for an older child can prove disastrous for a younger child. As my colleague and friend Dr. C. Everett Koop (U.S. Surgeon General) once said, "If a disease were killing our children in such proportions [as accidents are], people would be outraged and demand that this killer be stopped."

I encourage you to read this important book. By understanding the areas of danger that face your children indoors and outdoors, you are taking an important step in protecting your children and joining us in the fight against the leading killer of America's children.

MARTIN R. EICHELBERGER, M.D.
Director, Trauma Center
Children's Hospital
National Medical Center
Washington, D.C.

Introduction

After nine months of planning and anticipating your baby's birth, the moment arrives. Once outside the protective warmth of the womb he is your greatest joy, your greatest responsibility. In a few short months you'll become aware of just how monumental that responsibility is. You'll marvel at his unbridled energy, his overwhelming curiosity, his enormous capacity for turning your day into a nonstop battle for control. Sometime during this phase you will ask yourselves, "What have we done?"

What you have done is created a wonderful bundle of trouble, a tiny human capable of infinite bouts of trouble-making. Remember that sleepy-eyed, gurgling angel who sat passively in his infant seat for hours on end, playing with his toys and smiling serenely at you?

Now when you look down you catch only a blurred vision of your toddler breaking every known speed record to get down those stairs, to eat everything that isn't bolted down, to wash his overalls in the toilet, to climb Couch Everest, and on and on in a seemingly endless display of defiance and thirst for adventure. As he grows, the activities may change, but that spirit of adventure will not.

Your child's boundless enthusiasm and daredevil behavior may seem amusing, even entertaining, to the adults around him. But parents, beware. The possibilities for injury to your children are endless. Our homes present us with electrical, chemical, physical, and logistical hazards we need to identify and remove.

By educating yourself, using a little common sense, and practicing various techniques that we call "child-proofing," you can help overcome a majority of these potential dangers to your child. You stand between your child and the number one threat to his health: accidents.

Naturally, every small child will experience his share of cuts, bruises, and other minor mishaps along the way. But if you as a parent make yourself aware of potential trouble spots, of when an accident is likely to occur and how you can intervene, your child's chances of remaining accident-free will be greatly increased.

Over the last several years, accidents have replaced disease as the number-one killer of children. This news sounds alarming but there is a positive side to it: experts tell us that as many as nine out of ten of these accidents can be prevented.

How? By understanding what an accident is, when it is likely to occur, and how you can step in to halt the process. Accidents are not always the chance events we imagine them to be or are taught to believe they are. They occur for specific reasons, some of which are under our control.

An accident occurs as a result of a number of related factors leading in one unfortunate direction. If we know that leaving cleansers under the sink could lead to a poisoning episode, and if we know that the hours of 3 P.M. to 6 P.M. have proved to show a higher incidence of poisoning accidents, then why allow either of these high-risk situations to cause you anxiety? Knowing of a hazard can be the first step in removing it from your home. By removing the toxic cleanser from your child's reach you have eliminated the first factor in the progression.

Keeping in mind that the higher poisoning rates occur during the hours of 3 P.M. to 6 P.M., you can intervene by occupying your child with specific supervised projects that still allow you to carry on with your routine. You will then have eliminated the second factor in the progression.

When we speak about accidents involving children, we can become even more specific about the factors leading or contributing to those accidents. There are three basic factors that lend themselves to the progression or path of an accident:

• The child's developmental age. As we will discuss later in Chapter 1, each developmental stage poses its own unique set of potential hazards. A child's skills—social, motor, and language—all are contributing factors to what situation that child is capable of creating, and it could be a hazardous one.

• The physical or social situation the child may be in at the time of the potential accident. Naturally a child's environment—the complete physical space he occupies—is a source of concern. If there are certain aspects of the environment that could be considered unsafe, how can we be sure that an accident will not occur? By the same token, if the caregivers present are not fully prepared mentally for a possible accident, the result is all the more likely to be tragic.

• The actual about-to-occur event. At the very point at which the accident occurs, the imaginary "caution" boundary is crossed. The choice is made in a split second. How do we prevent that crossing-over?

Parents and responsible caregivers are in a position to intervene on behalf of a child in the battle against accidents. We have the ability to educate ourselves so that we can stand between our children and a potential accident. In order to do so properly we need to have three basic pieces of information:

- the child's age
- the hazards most likely to be met with at that stage, or at a particular time or situation
- the most effective way of intervening in a particular situation.

With all this knowledge at our disposal, what is the next step to intervention? There are several ways of actually becoming the intervening force, the best "safety device" for your child. (This is a concept we will deal with at length in Chapter 9.) They include:

- Protection: keeping your child and the potential hazard from coming together. One way to do this is to install safety devices, which this book will help you to do.

- Discipline: using consistent, fair means to ensure that certain household rules designed with child safety in mind are not broken on a regular basis.

- Regulation: responsible adults need to monitor and adjust their response to child behavior in order to intervene effectively. As a child grows, parents need to be willing to alter the method of intervention to provide the most effective guarantee against accidents. For instance, we would never allow a one-year-old to cross the street alone. But depending on the street and degree of activity on that street, we may be more likely to allow a supervised four-year-old to exercise his abilities.

- Teaching: By using words in combination with action, we can most effectively impart to our children the information we have about safety. If children are provided with safety learning experiences such as being taught how to cross the street, they often learn to make safe judgments by the time they are four or five. What they have learned about safety they need to practice in the presence of adults. As these same adults make suggestions regarding safety by explaining through words and action, a child will gain the self-confidence necessary to make those judgments on his own. Explanations are far more meaningful to a child than simply forbidding him to engage in a particular activity.

Remember that despite all these ways of coming between your child and impending hazards, there is still a child's natural curiosity to be dealt with. Overprotecting small children will only lead to stifling that urge to explore, and could make them fearful and shy. That is not our aim. We simply need to protect them from potential accidents while they learn to protect themselves. We are responsible ultimately for helping them to learn that lesson in a way which satisfies their curiosity in the safest possible manner.

So, how do we recognize all the potential physical and situational hazards? This book is designed to provide you with the necessary information. Written from a parent's point of view, by mothers who have spent the better part of the last several years raising small children, it is offered with the simple desire to see your children raised as happily and accident-free as ours have been.

We will touch on many areas of concern, including the commonest types of accidents involving children, and the types of safety devices available on the market and their effectiveness. We will also include a room-by-room checklist which helps you go through your home and examine specific problem areas as they pertain to each room. We offer the guidelines, suggestions, and resource lists you need to make yourself into the best "safety device" at your child's disposal.

Childproofing requires a little time and effort on your part but the results are well worth it. By childproofing your home before your child is mobile, you will have saved him from accidents you may not even have thought about. Remember, do not think of this as a permanent condition, either for your house or your child. Life will only be turned physically upside down for a few years.

As soon as your child has discovered that there is more to the world than Mom, Dad, and four walls, you will be free: free to put your prized antique vase back on the shelf and free to take possession of your home again. But until then . . . Don't waste a moment! That little dickens will be on the loose before you know it, and no one wants him to be another statistic. Open this book and childproof. Now! Use the knowledge to intervene on your child's behalf. Prevent accidents!

Chapter One
Avoiding Home Accidents

THE ACCIDENT CLIMATE

The first step in avoiding home accidents is knowing when they are more likely to occur. Certain situations and even various times of day have proved to show higher incidences of accidents. Accidents are more likely to occur:

☐ When the adults responsible for the care of the child do not understand what to expect in terms of behavior and capabilities of children at their various developmental stages.

☐ When a child is cared for by an adult who is unfamiliar with that child's routine and activities—e.g., a babysitter or visiting relative.

☐ When the family is economically or socially unstable.

☐ When the marital relationship of a child's parents is a tense one.

☐ When there are family conflicts such as death, divorce, illness.

☐ When there is a major change in the child's environment such as moving to a new house, changing day-care providers, etc.

☐ When a child's routine is not consistent.

☐ When a child's environment is full of hazards: toxic substances left within reach; easy access to the garage and other dangerous areas, etc.

☐ When there are no safe areas to play in.

☐ When children are not closely supervised.

☐ When the play space and equipment (toys, playground equipment, etc.) are not safe for a child's activities.

☐ When the dinner hour approaches (between 3 and 6 P.M.) Toward the end of the day, people are usually fatigued. A child may sense your diminished attention and may find ways to earn it back—not always in the safest way.

☐ As the week progresses, Thursday and Friday being especially prone, with Saturday being the worst day for accidents. Again the correlation between fatigue and a child's sense of your dwindling attention comes into play.

☐ When a child is hungry, tired, angry, or confused. The hour before mealtime shows a much higher incidence of poisoning than other times.

☐ When the child's mother is ill, pregnant, or menstruating.

Most of these factors fall under the category of common sense. Others may surprise you somewhat. But by far the one that will prove most significant in your attempts to protect your child is the first on the list. Understanding your child, her behavior, and her capabilities at each stage of her growth and development is an essential tool in the fight against accidents. Each stage brings with it a unique set of possibilities for accidents and a unique way of reducing those risks.

BIRTH TO FOUR MONTHS

The newborn is a helpless creature requiring constant and consistent care and protection. Her basic needs are food, being bathed, having diapers changed, and sleeping. It would seem then that this is a perfectly safe time in her young life. After all, where could an accident occur? The most a parent needs to be aware of is supporting her floppy head. Not true.

At this stage (as at all others), it is vitally important that your baby's rate of growth and development not be underestimated. A parent must always anticipate the unexpected. This awareness should tell you that at no time should an infant be left alone outside the confined areas of her crib or playpen.

SAFETY IN FEEDING

Being fed is perhaps the greatest source of pleasure for an infant. As a result, as soon as she is able, everything finds its way into her mouth. Parents must then start being cautious about objects within the baby's reach that she could choke on. Toys that have buttons for eyes, unacceptably small rattles, and tiny objects hiding in the nap of carpeting, to name a few, are all potential hazards and should promptly be removed or disposed of entirely.

While bottle-feeding your baby, remember these simple points:

● Avoid bottle propping. Your baby will be more comfortable resting in your arms, and the likelihood of inhaling regurgitated liquid will be lessened.

● Make sure the nipple opening is adequate for your baby's needs. If it is too large, excess liquid may cause the baby to gag.

SAFETY IN CHANGING

If you have never seen your baby roll over (usually beginning at about three months of age), it is much easier to understand why you wouldn't hesitate to leave her unstrapped on the changing table to look for a clean diaper or disposable towelette. Please beware. She might choose that very instant to exhibit her newly acquired skill. Sadly, many infants have sustained crippling injuries, even death as the result of a fall. Remember when changing:

● Always use a safety strap if you have a nursery changing table. Whether or not you have a safety strap, keep one hand on the baby at all times and if the article you require is not within reach, take the baby with you. There are many commercial straps available on the market.

● Try and keep everything handy so you will not have to interrupt the diaper changing.

● Remember, the middle of your bed is not the safest place either! The floor is.

● If the phone or doorbell rings during changing you can ignore it, place the baby in the safety of the crib, or take the baby with you.

SAFETY IN BATHING

Here are some points for you to consider:

● Make sure the bathwater is a comfortable temperature. Use your elbow to determine this.

• Under no circumstances should your baby ever be left alone in the bathtub.

• It may be a good idea to take the phone off the hook or turn on the answering machine. The temptation to answer a ringing phone is sometimes too great.

• Disregard ringing doorbells, or wrap your baby warmly and take her with you.

• Keep the bottom of the tub or sink lined with a suitable non-slip mat. If your baby is still in an infant tub, an ordinary bath towel will serve nicely. There are also a number of foam or sponge mats available on the market.

• Support the baby firmly.

OTHER PRECAUTIONS

Always use the safety straps on infant seats, strollers, and high chairs, taking the time to make sure they are fastened correctly and are in good working order.

SIDS PREVENTION

Sudden Infant Death Syndrome (SIDS) most frequently affects infants between two and four months of age, although the first year is a general-risk guideline. Since the exact cause of "crib death" is still unknown, it is important to heed the safety information that is available.

• Know CPR before your child is born. You will be prepared to respond if your child stops breathing.

• Consult your pediatrician if your infant develops a bad cold or respiratory distress. Report any episodes of interrupted breathing that concern you.

• Feed your child properly! Do not leave your child alone in a crib with a bottle.

- Dress your child in loose clothing for sleeping.
- Keep stuffed animals, pillows, and extra blankets out and away from the crib.
- Maintain a well-ventilated environment for your sleeping baby (even in the car).

FOUR TO SEVEN MONTHS

At this stage your child still requires constant attention. Accidents can occur with greater frequency during these months as your child becomes more mobile and starts grasping for objects.

Perhaps the most potentially dangerous of these new movements is her ability to roll over from her stomach to her back. When left unattended in a crib containing blankets, pillows, soft stuffed toys or clothing, she could roll into one of these items and suffocate. A child of this age is not physically able to remove the offending article and may panic. The feeling has been likened to an adult losing orientation underwater and not being able to perceive the direction of the surface.

The second potentially dangerous new movement is the grasping of objects. It is only a step from grasping an object to placing that object in the mouth. Needless to say the results can be deadly.

Remember these important points:

- All potentially suffocating articles should be removed from the crib.
- The crib mattress should be firm so that the baby's face does not settle too deeply into it.
- All bumper pads should be fastened securely to the sides and corners of the crib.

• Under no circumstances should you leave your baby unattended on a bed, couch, changing table, or any other high location.

• Be very careful to keep choking hazards or otherwise harmful objects out of your baby's reach. Check the floors and carpeting and underneath furniture frequently for such objects.

SEVEN TO TWELVE MONTHS

At this point, if you have not completed your room-by-room tour and child-proofed accordingly, we suggest you do so because the age of seven to twelve months is a time of great curiosity for your child. Everything makes its way into her mouth and while she can pull herself up quite well, she can also pull everything down with equal proficiency.

Among the major developmental milestones:

Eight months: Looks for an object which has fallen from her grasp.

Nine months: Can pull herself up on her knees, then to her feet, and then can stand with a handhold.

Ten months: Can stand fairly well and can manage a few steps with a handhold.

Eleven months: Can stand all alone for a short period of time. If she falls to a sitting position, she can pull herself to her feet again.

Obviously these stages are general ones and your baby may not necessarily fall into any of them at the specified time. But nonetheless this period is one of rapid physical development and brings with it a number of potential hazards. Increased mobility will pose threatening situations if you do not intervene.

Remember these important points:

- All choking hazards must be removed from within reach. If she drops her toy and starts looking for it, you do not want her finding loose change or matches under the couch.

- Because she is reaching, tie up loose cords; remove easily toppled lamps and similar objects; keep hot foods and drinks out of reach. Keep pot handles turned toward the back of the stove.

- Because she is walking, keep floors clear of clutter.

- Because everything goes into her mouth, be extremely aware of medicines and cleaning materials. Keep them well away from foods. Keep these toxins locked and out of her reach.

ONE TO THREE YEARS

At this stage your child's enormous curiosity, coupled with greatly increased motor development, make for serious accident potential. A child of this age rarely comprehends danger and will engage in an activity quickly with no thought of the consequences. Your job of intervention will take on a new dimension here: language. Even though you may have been using language as a tool all along, only now will it start to show its effectiveness. It is time to begin teaching verbal lessons. But please remember that language must be coupled with action. A toddler is not developed enough to relate the words to the action herself. A parent must step in, use the instructive language and physically display the correct behavior, remove the hazard, or remove the child from the hazard. Whatever the case, never waver. Consistency is the key to making sure the lessons are absorbed for later reference.

In terms of developmental milestones, watch for:

Twelve months: Can pull herself to her feet and walk with a handhold.

Fifteen months: Can walk alone, bending down to pick up fallen objects.

Eighteen months: Can walk alone well, negotiating stairs.

Nineteen months: Can run and imitate single movements and may follow single directions.

Naturally, a toddler will be able to do all of the above with greater proficiency as the months progress.

Remember these important points:

• Teach important safety lessons by using both words and actions.

• Use gates at the head and foot of stairways.

• Play areas should contain only safe equipment and should be fenced in. (See Chapter 6 for more information.)

• Teach the meaning of "hot" by using the word consistently and demonstrate the kinds of things that are hot.

• Keep all toxic substances out of reach, preferably locked away and out of view.

• Toddlers have a tendency to imitate our activity as they grow older. Keep all knives secured, smoking materials out of reach, and so forth. Examine your own habits!

• Be cautious and aware of the toys you allow your children to play with. Are they age-appropriate? (See Chapter 5.)

THREE TO FIVE YEARS

At this stage curiosity is overwhelming and your child will not be content with the confines of her own house and yard. She is ready to explore the world. Deal with this enthusiasm accordingly by allowing freedom, but also by setting very definite guidelines for safe behavior. This will be discussed in greater length and detail in Chapter 8.

What is essential to remember once again is that words and action go hand in hand to create the most easily absorbed safety lessons. It is not enough to tell your five-year-old to wear her seat belt. You must show her the soundness of the safety message by using yours as well.

Make sure that your disciplinary guidelines are well established so that a child knows what behavior is expected of her and the consequences of not adhering to the code of behavior you have established. Consistency is vital.

COMMON ACCIDENTS BY AGE

In case we haven't already made you aware of the most common dangers, we have listed below the specific types of accidents that occur most frequently at certain age levels. Although they are not listed in a particular order, it is wise to keep in mind that the automobile is the leading cause of death or injury to children of *all* ages.

Birth to six months:
- automobile accidents
- diaper-changing table falls
- bathwater burns
- crib accidents

Six to twelve months:
- automobile accidents
- falls against sharp furniture
- electric burns from chewing on appliance cords

- toy-related injuries
- high chair/walker/stroller accidents

One to two years:
- automobile accidents
- exploring/climbing accidents
- cuts (usually from knives)
- eating poisonous plants
- drowning from unguarded water hazards (pools, ponds, wells, etc.)

Three to five years:
- automobile accidents
- tricycle/bicycle accidents
- yard and street accidents
- playground accidents
- fire accidents
- drowning from unguarded water hazards

We have put you on the launching pad with this chapter by letting you know the possibilities. Now you will learn the practical aspects of intervention. It's time to put these words into action.

Chapter Two
Child Safety Devices

In the past few years there has been an explosion of child-proofing devices available on the market. By "devices" we mean the countless gadgets manufactured by toy companies, child safety product companies, hardware manufacturers, and so on, that are designed to protect your child in a number of dangerous situations.

There are several basic categories of these safety devices:

- car seats
- electronic devices and intercoms designed to help you tend your baby from a distance
- electrical safety devices
- gates
- harnesses
- kits containing a variety of safety products in one package
- padding/covering devices to protect children from blows sustained during a fall against sharp edges
- safety latches and closures to prevent opening cabinets, cupboards, doors, and drawers
- miscellaneous items ranging from sunshades for the car to rearview mirror extenders

The basic premise behind all these products is that they will protect your child and keep him from exploring potential danger zones. When used properly, some devices do help parents with the task of childproofing. Unfortunately, many manufacturers neglect to tell parents of the drawbacks to various devices. They play on our guilt with slick advertising and the notion that without their products we will fail to keep our children safe from accidents. This is not true. For almost every device on the market there is a simple alternative which can be more effective. We will discuss this at length later in the chapter. If you do plan on installing any of these devices in your home, there are a few things to be kept in mind.

How many of us have gone to our local retailers looking for safety devices only to be met with an entire wallful of products, many of which look the same, many of which look impossible to figure out? How do you choose? This is definitely a problem. Countless parents spend time picking out what they think is the device best suited for their home only to bring it home, attempt to install it, and discover that (a) it does not fit the area to be childproofed; (b) it does not function properly; (c) it breaks when they try to install it; or (d) it only lasts a few short weeks under the strain of a curious toddler's probings even if it is properly installed. These are the shortcomings.

Perhaps the worst of these shortcomings is the very short life-span of many of the devices, either because of a lack of durability or because a child can soon figure out how to operate them. At some point, usually sooner than you expect, your child will become quite adept at dismantling your efforts to keep him safe. The doorknob cover will come off with the flick of a finger, the toilet latch will disappear in a flush, and the Velcro hinge will become just another item in the junk drawer.

We cannot let ourselves become less attentive just because we have installed devices. Sure, you can ease up for a while, secure in the knowledge that little fingers will not insert car keys into the electrical outlet if it is capped, but there will come a day when those caps can and very well may be removed by those same little fingers.

The same is true for many of the devices. Do not take their usefulness for granted. Do not let your parental guard down because you have installed twelve dollars' worth of hardware. They are meant to *help* with the job of protecting your child. But, as we have already mentioned, they cannot be the primary intervening force between your child and an accident. That is your function as a parent.

As for recognizing which of the products are best suited for your needs, read the packaging carefully before buying an item, and if you do choose to purchase a particular device and find that it does not live up to its promise, return it to the retailer and follow up with a letter to the manufacturer. Only by informing them of any problems can they develop better, more effective safety products.

Child safety devices can be purchased in many places these days including toy, drug, hardware, department, grocery, baby specialty stores and through a number of mail order catalogues. If you have trouble finding any, the following information may help you.

The lists that follow offer a brief description of the various safety devices and how they function, the method of installation, any shortcomings, recommended alternatives, and charts* for brand comparison.

Remember, new and hopefully better devices are cropping up on the market all the time. Be aware as a consumer and parent interested in child safety.

CAR SEATS

TYPES AVAILABLE:

☐ Infant   ☐ Boosters
☐ Toddler ☐ Convertibles

INTENDED FUNCTION:

To secure children in the car properly. It is the most lifesaving device available. No parent should be without a car seat of some kind. In most states car seat use is mandated by law for all children traveling in cars who weigh less than 40 pounds or are under four years of age. Each of the four kinds is designed for children of a specific developmental age.

☐ Infant. For use from birth to 20 pounds; rearward-facing only.

☐ Toddler. For children weighing over 20 pounds (or

---

* The ratings on the charts that follow represent the authors' opinions and are based solely upon home tests conducted by the authors over a period of several months. The devices were tested on children ranging in age from birth to age five. While every effort was made to examine the devices using a uniform method, the ratings are of necessity somewhat subjective.

KinderKraft, Inc., listed on the device charts for child safety sample kits, padding and covering devices, and harnesses, is owned and operated by the authors.

CAR SEATS

TYPE	MANUFACTURER	AVG. PRICE	RATING	COMMENTS
Infant Infant Car Seat 580	Century Products, Inc. Gerber Products Co. 1366 Commerce Dr. Stow, OH 44224	$40	★★★★	Lift-out car seat that removes from base for use as carrier. Two harness positions.
Infant/Swing/Carrier 915	Evenflo 1801 Commerce Dr. P.O. Box 1217 Piqua, OH 45356	$75	★★★★	This infant swing has a detachable seat that doubles as a car seat. FAA-approved for air travel.
Toddler Century 3000STE	Century Products, Inc. Gerber Products Co. 1366 Commerce Dr. Stow, OH 44224	$80	★★★★	One-strap shield and harness. Fantasy simulated control panel for the playful traveler.

Product	Manufacturer	Price	Rating	Features
Booster Cosco Explorer 1	Cosco, Inc., Juvenile Products 2525 State St. Columbus, IN 47201	$33	★★★	Side pivot, self-adjusting shield. Provides height options for the growing child.
Convertible Century 2000STE	Century Products, Inc. Gerber Products Co. 1366 Commerce Dr. Stow, OH 44224	$90	★★★★	3-point harness, body pad, straps that adjust easily.
Ultra Ride	Kolocraft 5430 E. Union Pacific Ave. Los Angeles, CA 90040	$80	★★★★	5-point harness, reclines and is FAA-approved for air travel.
Fisher-Price Car Seat*	Fisher-Price 636 Girard Ave. East Aurora, NY 14052	$110	★★★★	3-point retractable harness that locks snugly.
Cosco Commuter Seat	Cosco Inc., Juvenile Products 2525 State St. Columbus, IN 47201	$70	★★★	3-point harness with shield. One-step buckle.

*If you have an older model Fisher-Price car seat without a button stop on one of the shoulder straps, call 1-800-828-7315.

RATING SCALE KEY ★★★★ excellent ★★★ good ★★ average ★ poor

when a child can sit up comfortably). For use facing forward.

☐ Boosters. Designed for children 30 to 70 pounds. Not a necessity. Seat belts are sufficient at either 40 pounds or four years of age.

☐ Convertibles. The most practical design. Can be adapted for children from birth to 43 pounds. Rear-facing for infants; forward-facing for toddlers.

HOW TO INSTALL:

Each seat has its own method of installation. The majority involve using your car's seat belts. Read the instructions carefully and have the seat installed before your child is born or the adoption papers are signed.

SHORTCOMINGS:

Check secondhand car seats carefully. All car seats made after 1981 meet federal safety standards. If you have any questions, consult the Resources guide (Appendix 4) and contact the appropriate authorities. Car seats, properly used, can prevent 80 to 90 percent of automobile fatalities and injuries to children.

ALTERNATIVES:

There are none! The most dangerous place for a child or infant in a car is on the lap or in the arms of an adult. Often car accidents are not in your control. The majority of accidents in which children are killed are caused by the driver of the other vehicle. Do not bend your rules. Remember, most fatal accidents involving children occur on routine trips, under normal driving conditions, close to home.

(Note about the Rating Scale. The variety of car seats available today is seemingly unlimited. We have listed only a few popular models that meet current safety standards. Many outstanding car seats come and go on the market. If you desire a more comprehensive shopping guide, contact the American Academy of Pediatrics at (800)-336-5475, the National Passenger Safety Association at (202) 429-0515, or your local automobile association.)

ELECTRONIC DEVICES AND INTERCOMS

TYPES AVAILABLE:

☐ Beepers   ☐ Intercoms
☐ Alarms

INTENDED FUNCTION:

☐ Beepers: These devices are comparable to those carried by physicians. The parent wears a small electronic device which responds to the counterpart worn by the child. If the child wanders more than approximately 20 feet from the parent an alarm will sound to alert the adult. Older children can also alert parents if need be.

☐ Alarms: A sounding electronic beeper informing us that a certain door or cabinet has been invaded by the "family genius." Pool alarms warn of pool area entry.

☐ Intercoms: These devices allow parents to hear from a distance what a child is doing in another room. They are usually portable so that, for example, if Dad is outside with one intercom, watering the lawn, when your baby wakes from her nap in a room with the other intercom, he will be able to hear her stirring and respond.

ELECTRONIC DEVICES AND INTERCOMS

TYPE	MANUFACTURER	AVG. PRICE	RATING	COMMENTS
Alarms Don't Touch the Portable Safety Alarm	Kwik Find, Ltd. 25 Tiburon St. San Rafael, CA 94901	$7	★★	Sticks on drawers or cabinets. 60-day warranty. Not enough protection to keep kids away from toxins. Useful as a warning device in large homes. Uses a battery.
Gerry Baby Safetronics Door Alert	Gerry Baby Products Gerico Inc. 12520 Grant Dr. P.O. Box 33755 Denver, CO 80233	$9	★★	Sticks or screws on doors. Useful while traveling, and on doors leading to the outside, downstairs, or ''off limits'' areas. Parents tend to gain a false sense of security with its use. Uses batteries.

Remington Pool Alarm	Remington Products 60 Main St. Bridgeport, CT 06602	$100	★★★	Alarm sounds when children or pets fall in the pool. Birds can easily trigger this device. Battery operated.
Beepers The Nanny Electronic Babysitter	Kwik Find, Ltd. 25 Tiburon St. San Rafael, CA 94901	$10	★	Appears to encourage parents to allow their toddler to explore public places. Unreliable.
Toddler Alert	Safe-T-Guard Nasta Industries Inc. 200 5th Ave. New York, NY 10010	$12.50	★	Same.
Intercoms Fisher-Price Nursery Monitor	Fisher-Price 636 Girard Ave. East Aurora, NY 14052	$44	★★★	Good choice for a large home. Only monitor advertising limited 1-year warranty.

RATING SCALE KEY ★★★★ excellent ★★★ good ★★ average ★ poor

TYPE	MANUFACTURER	AVG. PRICE	RATING	COMMENTS
Gerry Baby Safetronics Baby Intercom	Gerry Baby Products Gerico Inc. 12520 Grant Dr. P.O. Box 33755 Denver, CO 80233	$38	★★	Smallest model listed.
Little Listener	ERTL Kiddie, Inc. Hwy. 20 and 136 Dyersville, IA 52040	$49.50	★★	Decorative doll figure for the nursery.
Baby Minder	Safe-T-Guard Nasta Industries, Inc. 200 5th Ave. New York, NY 10010	$25	★★	Available in standard or decorative models.
Teddy Care Dual Nursery Lamp and Monitor	Cosco, Inc. Juvenile Products 2525 State St. Columbus, IN 47201	$76.50	★★	Serves two functions: decorative lamp and monitor.

RATING SCALE KEY ★★★★ excellent ★★★ good ★★ average ★ poor

HOW TO INSTALL:

These are portable devices and can be carried from room to room as needed. They usually require batteries.

SHORTCOMINGS:

☐ Beepers:

- They are advertised for toddlers but may be more suitable for older children because parents should not allow their toddlers to wander.
- A toddler might find these devices more of an amusement than a precaution. Can't you just see your two-year-old tormenting you with the "beep-beep-beep" as he stalks the toy department?
- In our home test they did not prove very reliable.

☐ Alarms:

- Not really practical. They too may become an annoying toy to gain a parent's attention.
- Pool alarms can be set off frequently by stray animals.

☐ Intercoms:

- Going beyond a certain distance will cause their usefulness to diminish.
- They may cause you to let down your guard in terms of checking on your baby.

ALTERNATIVES:

These are not true safety devices but, rather, helpful tools. We believe the best alternative is, quite simply, close parental supervision. Try a bell tied around the doorknob or a fence gate to sound a more pleasant alarm.

ELECTRICAL SAFETY DEVICES

TYPES AVAILABLE:

- ☐ Electrical outlet caps
- ☐ Electrical outlet covers
- ☐ Cord shorteners
- ☐ Cord guards
- ☐ Safety disks
- ☐ Dimmers and night lights

INTENDED FUNCTION:

☐ Electrical outlet caps: These are small plastic two-pronged objects that fit directly into unused electrical sockets and prevent children from inserting anything.

☐ Electrical outlet covers: These are larger devices designed to fit over the entire wall plate. Their secondary purpose is to allow for more flexibility in terms of using the sockets. The covers hold plugs and cord in place, preventing children from yanking the electrical cord out of the wall. All varieties screw into the wall plate, but twist and snap-on designs allow for easy access. Other less practical varieties are permanently installed and must be unscrewed using a screwdriver every time a plug is engaged or disengaged. This variety is best used for sockets kept permanently in use. Most likely to hold a stereo, TV, or lamp cord in place.

☐ Cord shorteners: To take up the slack of appliance cords, to keep little hands and feet from pulling on or tripping over them.

☐ Cord guards: These devices secure the cord to an end table. Their main function is to prevent small children from pulling lamps to the floor.

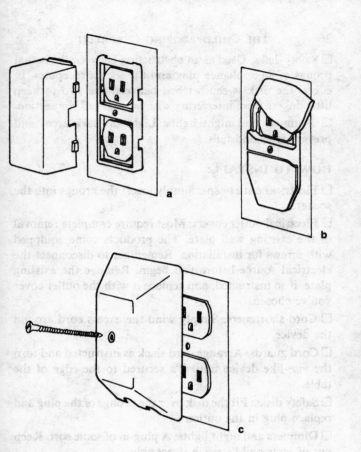

Outlet Covers

a. snap-on   b. spring-loaded   c. screw-in

☐ Safety disks: Used as an obstruction between the actual prongs of an appliance plug and the socket receptors. In effect, the disk is sandwiched between the two to keep little fingers from interfering with an engaged connection.

☐ Dimmers and night lights: Light up dark areas and prevent trips and falls.

HOW TO INSTALL:

☐ Electrical outlet caps: Simply insert the prongs into the socket.

☐ Electrical outlet covers: Most require complete removal of the existing wall plate. The products come equipped with screws for installation. Remember to disconnect the electrical source before you begin. Remove the existing plate, if so instructed, and replace it with the outlet cover you've chosen.

☐ Cord shorteners: Simply wind the excess cord around the device.

☐ Cord guards: Arrange cord slack as instructed and turn the vise-like device until it's secured to the edge of the table.

☐ Safety disks: Fit the disk over the prongs of the plug and replace plug in the outlet.

☐ Dimmers and night lights: A plug-in of some sort. Keep out of your child's reach if possible.

SHORTCOMINGS:

☐ Electrical outlet caps:

- They are difficult to remove should you need to use the outlet. Once removed, they are often misplaced, leaving an exposed receptacle.
- They are small enough to present a choking hazard.

- Occasionally, they are too loose-fitting to be practical.
- Not all varieties are made of UL-approved plastic materials.

□ Electrical outlet covers:

Snap-on/Swivel cap design

- A child could knock the cover off with a heavy object, but this is not likely.
- Confusion may result when examining the various models available and trying to purchase the one that best suits your needs.

Screw-on design

- It is inconvenient to have to unscrew the device with a screwdriver each time you want to use plugs.
- Some appliance plugs have a long stem and will not fit into this cover.
- The screw-on variety poses a fire hazard if accidentally knocked off the wall. It tends to pull the entire electrical box out of the wall.

Spring-loaded

- These gadgets flip open a door, allowing parents to engage the plug. Unfortunately, children love to play with snapping gadgets, making this more of an attraction than a safety device.

Twisting

- Not worth the expense when they serve the same function as a simple outlet cap.

- The twisting holes are a risk if your child fiddles with the device.

☐ Cord shorteners:

- An unnecessary expense.

☐ Cord guards:

- Bulky, attention-drawing device.
- Proper installation does not always ensure effective functioning.

☐ Safety disks:

- They don't work! Because they are so thick, they often do not allow for an adequate connection to be made between the appliance and socket and will cause the plug to insert only partially. You would then have an exposed live connection which could prove very harmful.

☐ Dimmers and night lights:

- Lights placed in low receptacles attract little ones. The attraction is more of a hazard than darkness.

ALTERNATIVES:

☐ Electrical outlet caps and covers:

- Furniture may be placed strategically in front of outlets. But remember, all must be guarded somehow.
- A little electrical or plastic tape may be placed over the receptacle (especially useful if you are traveling).

☐ Cord shorteners:

- A twist tie found in your package of plastic garbage bags or grocery produce section will work just as

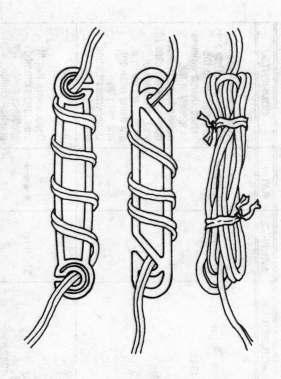

Cord Shorteners

Cord shorteners are designed to take up slack neatly on hanging electrical cords that may pose a tripping or chewing hazard.

effectively. Simply roll up the excess cord and twist the tie around it.

- Cords can be secured to the floor or wall with strong adhesive tape.
- Tuck cords neatly behind furniture if possible.
- When an appliance is not in use, unplug it and place the cord out of reach.

ELECTRICAL SAFETY DEVICES

TYPE	MANUFACTURER	AVG. PRICE	RATING	COMMENTS
Electrical Outlet Caps	Gerber Products Co. 445 State St. Fremont, MI 49412	$1.50 up	★★★★	Avoid the varieties with designs. They are an attraction to the hazard. Some varieties fit loosely in the outlets found in older homes. Gerber caps fit well, are made of translucent material, are flame retardant, and carry an Underwriters Listing (UL).
Electrical Outlet Covers *Snap-on/Swivel-cap* Shockblockers	Tots World Co. P.O. Box 148 Blue Bell, PA 19422	$1.50 up	★★★	Deep covers that fit over long-stemmed appliance cords. The practical choice.

Outlet Cover	Gerber Products Co. 445 State St. Fremont, MI 49412	$2.50 up	★★★★	Similar design. White.
KidPruf 1 & 2	KidPruf America, Inc. 15 Central Way Suite 1 Kirkland, WA 98033	$3.50 up	★★★★	Unique patented design made of UL-approved plastic materials. Expensive choice that is not a necessity for each outlet in your home. Various KidPruf designs make purchase choice difficult.
Permanent Screw-on				
Plug Guard	Robin Industries 7455 West State Road 2 La Porte, IN 46350	$1 up	★★	You will spot many taped-up packages on your store shelves. They do not always fit over engaged plugs. An impractical choice. Available in 4 colors.

TYPE	MANUFACTURER	AVG. PRICE	RATING	COMMENTS
Twist	Sanitoy, Inc. Nursery Needs Nursery Lane P.O. Box 2167 Fitchburg, MA 01420	$1.50 up	★★	Does not lock plug in place. Good to use on an outlet you use frequently for vacuuming or kitchen appliances.
Spring-loaded				
Socket-Lock-it	Enex Corp. P.O. Box 2143 Farmington Hills, MI 48018	$1.50	★	Not recommended. Poses an unnecessary attraction.
Care Bears Safety Night Light	William F. B. Johnson Co. 901 East Luzerne St. Philadelphia, PA 19124	$4	★	Same. Care Bear designs add even more attraction to the hazard.
Cord Shorteners	The First Years One Kiddie Dr. Avon, MA 02322	$1 up	★★	Neat but unnecessary way to shorten cord slack.

Product	Company	Price	Rating	Comments
Cord Guards	Playskool Hasbro, Inc. 433 Shaker Rd. East Longmeadow, MA 01028	$4	★★	An expensive solution. Bulky and unattractive. Try rearranging the hazard instead.
Safety Discs	Baby and Child 7 Shadow Ct. Owings Mills, MD 21117	$2	★	Unnecessary. May pose even a greater hazard in some homes.
Dimmers and Night Lights Musical Light Dimmer	Fisher-Price 636 Girard Ave. East Aurora, NY 14052	$19.50 up	★★★	Needs to be placed out of child's reach.
Slumber Lite	KinderGard 14822 Venture Dr. Dallas, TX 75234	$8	★	Light activated by your child's sounds. Annoying if your child is up a lot. May help a frightened child navigate to the bathroom with ease.

RATING SCALE KEY ★★★★ excellent ★★★ good ★★ average ★ poor

☐ Cord guards:

- Move the table lamp.
- Arrange the cord out of reach, tie up excess slack, and secure it in place between the wall and table.

☐ Safety disks:

- Don't waste your money!

☐ Dimmers and night lights:

- No light and the commitment to keeping floors picked up at night.
- Or, a hall light or lamp that you flip manually when nighttime roving is necessary.

GATES

TYPES AVAILABLE:

☐ Permanently installed (screwed into the wall)
☐ Pressure gates (can easily be moved from room to room)

INTENDED FUNCTION:

To keep your child out of dangerous or unsupervised areas. Usually used at the top or bottom (or both) of a stairway.

HOW TO INSTALL:

A gate can either be fastened in place by following specific directions and using a drill and screws or by pressure. The pressure gates require no drilling; rather, the two sides adjust to provide for easy installation and removal. Use only gates with straight top edges, small sturdy mesh or slats with no more than three inches between bars.

SHORTCOMINGS:

☐ Permanently installed:

- They take time to install and are less convenient to move from room to room.
- With the screw-in variety you need to find a beam or use molly bolts to assure proper installation.
- They do not always adjust to fit the doorway you need to block. Measure your doorway before shopping and check the adjustable measurements of a gate before your purchase.
- Do not work on wrought-iron balusters.

☐ Pressure Gates:

- It may be easier for a child to push against it and knock it down.
- Parents tend not to readjust and/or install it properly after each removal.
- They do not always adjust to fit the width of the area that needs to be blocked. Know the correct measurements before you purchase the gate.
- They do not always work on stairways with balusters.

ALTERNATIVES:

- Block undesirable areas with non-climbable furniture such as screens or a mattress.
- Take the time to consistently keep all doors to unsafe rooms closed.
- Post a sign to serve as a reminder.
- Have a custom gate built.

GATES

TYPE	MANUFACTURER	AVG. PRICE	RATING	COMMENTS
Permanently Installed				
Nu-Line	Nu-line Industries 214 Heasley St. Suring, WI 54174	$14	★★★	Model #1048 fits spaces up to 48" wide. Wood.
Gerry 505	Gerry Baby Products Gerico Inc. 12520 Grant Dr. P.O. Box 33755 Denver, CO 80233	$9	★★★	Plastic.
Worldbest	Worldbest Industries, Inc. 5025 S. Packard Ave. Cudany, WI 53110	$10 up	★★	A few inches higher than most. Fits openings 27" to 47" wide.

Pressure Gates			
Supergate III	North States Industries, Inc. 3650 Fremont Ave. N. Minneapolis, MN 55412	$19.50	★★★	Has sockets for added security. Fits spaces up to 42" wide. Will work on wrought-iron railings.
Century Gateway	Century Products, Inc. Gerber Products Co. 1366 Commerce Dr. Stow, OH 44224	$27	★★★	Has a walk-through double doorway design. Fits openings 27" to 36" wide.
Mapes 13321	Mapes Industries 6 Grace Ave. Great Neck, NY 11021	$14	★★	Tends to hold setting when gate is removed—easier reinstallation.

RATING SCALE KEY ★★★★ excellent ★★★ good ★★ average ★ poor

- Use a playpen or a larger enclosure. Portable play yards are available with areas up to 27 square feet to allow small children the safety of a playpen with more room to move around.

HARNESSES

TYPES AVAILABLE:

☐ Wrist ☐ Torso
☐ Straps and shopping cart devices

INTENDED FUNCTION:

Wrist and torso harnesses are used to physically attach parent and child. This is not a bad idea if your child tends to wander away and you find yourself in a busy shopping mall or airport. Straps are used in public high chairs or grocery carts along with specially designed shopping cart harnesses.

HOW TO INSTALL:

☐ Wrist: Simply attach one end of the tethering device to the parent's wrist and the other to the child's. The adjoining cord will tug when your child wanders off too far. Some parents choose to attach their end to their belt, handbag, or stroller.

☐ Torso: This harness fits like a jacket (without sleeves) attached to a "leash" which can be placed around the parent's wrist, handbag, or belt.

☐ Straps and shopping cart devices: They have simple fasteners. However, there are varieties of walking harnesses that also can serve the function of shopping cart restraint by attaching harness clips to the cart.

SHORTCOMINGS:

☐ Wrist:

- The wristbands are often kept closed by Velcro. At an early stage in your child's development, usually the time when you need them most, twelve to twenty-four months, they will be able to remove their side quite expertly. The same is true of the elasticized version.
- Children often balk at this kind of restraint. If you do opt for it, get them used to it early and be consistent with its use.

☐ Torso:

- This type usually involves an adjustment period for your child.
- The leash offers very little flexibility.

☐ Shopping cart harnesses and straps:

- They assure safety but are often left at home or in the car.
- Often an unnecessary expense because many stores now provide child safety straps upon request.

ALTERNATIVES:

In theory, beepers serve the same purpose by monitoring your child's whereabouts. We feel that a "holding hands" rule works equally well. If possible, shop without the baby or use a shopping service to reduce stress during the difficult years.

HARNESSES

TYPE	MANUFACTURER	AVG. PRICE	RATING	COMMENTS
Wrist	W. E. Care Co. Rte. 2, Box 8 Bellaire, MI 49615	$6 up	★★	Avoid Velcro closure on child wrist strap. Useful for older children who want to cooperate at crowded airports or public events.
Torso	Zip-a-Babe Life Manufacturing Co. East Boston, MA 02128	$7 up	★★★	Useful for the uncontrollable toddler as a walking harness, shopping cart strap, or high-chair restraint. Can be very frustrating at first for both child and parent.

Shopping Cart Harnesses and Straps			
Safety Strap	KinderKraft 501 N. Jefferson St. Arlington, VA 22205	$5.50	★★★	Handcrafted, padded strap. Easy to store in purse or pocket.
Shopping Cart Infant/child convertible	Carta-Kid The Great Kid Co. P.O. Box 654 Lexington, MA 02173	$15	★★★	If you use one, the convertible design is a better choice.
Shopping Cart	Whimsicality R.D. 2 (East Barre) Barre, VT 05641	$8	★★	Bulky and impractical unless you carry a diaper bag with you everywhere you go.

RATING SCALE KEY ★★★★ excellent ★★★ good ★★ average ★ poor

TYPE	MANUFACTURER	AVG. PRICE	RATING	COMMENTS
Bike Carrier Seat Harness	All American Products 2011 Swanson Court Gurnee, IL 60031	$6 up	★★★	Most bicycle child carriers already have an adequate harness. This shoulder harness is an added safety design.
Sling seats	Pride & Joy, Inc. P.O. Box 10156 St. Petersburg, FL 33733	$7.50 up	★★	Fabric harnesses. They can fit on the back of most frame chairs. Sew-yourself patterns are available. Outgrown quickly.

RATING SCALE KEY ★★★★ excellent ★★★ good ★★ average ★ poor

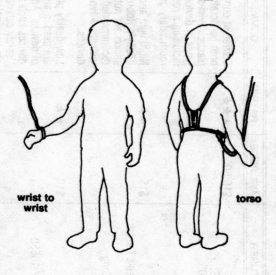

wrist to wrist

torso

Harnesses

Harnesses are designed to allow small children the freedom to walk without holding hands. A torso design is well suited to offer maximum protection to younger children, while the wrist design is better suited to older children, who are more likely to understand the importance of staying close.

CHILD SAFETY SAMPLE KITS

TYPE	MANUFACTURER	AVG. PRICE	RATING	COMMENTS
The Babyproofing Kit	KinderKraft, Inc. 501 N. Jefferson St. Arlington, VA 22205	$16.50	★★★	Starter kit containing both handcrafted and plastic devices. 8 types of devices including a room-by-room safety guide.
L'il Tots Child Home Safety Set	ENGO Industries Room 701, Peninsula Centre Tsimsha tsui East KowLoon, Hong Kong	$15	★★	Night light and "Baby's Room" sticker are not recommended. The kit includes 9 types of devices.
48-piece Child Protection Kit	Lillian Vernon 510 S. Fulton Ave. Mount Vernon, NY 10550	$10	★★	Low-quality plastics are used in all 8 types of devices. Adhesive devices such as "safety cabinet lock" are unreliable.

				Description
KinderGard Child Protection Kit and Sampler	KinderGard 14822 Venture Drive Dallas, TX 75234	$10	★★	Kit includes 4 types of devices in bulk quantities. Sampler includes examples of 6 types of devices. Includes home guide and 30-day limited warranty.
Safety Start Sets	Sanitoy, Inc. Nursery Needs Nursery Lane P.O. Box 2167 Fitchburg, MA 01420	$5 up	★★	Numerous manufacturers package a range of safety devices. Usually 4 or 5 types included per package.
Playskool Baby Guards House Set	Playskool Baby Hasbro, Inc. 108 Fairway Ct. Northvale, NJ 07647	$20	★★	Unique variety of 8 types of devices. Adhesive latches have a short life span.

RATING SCALE KEY   ★★★★ excellent   ★★★ good   ★★ average   ★ poor

CHILD SAFETY SAMPLE KITS

TYPES AVAILABLE:

☐ Starter kits containing a sample of several products
☐ Larger kits containing bulk quantities of popular devices

INTENDED FUNCTION:

To provide a number of child safety products in one convenient package.

HOW TO INSTALL:

All kits come with instructions for each particular item.

SHORTCOMINGS:

- They are often quite expensive.
- Many of the products may not be well suited to your home.
- They may offer too many of one device and not enough of another.
- The quality of the products may not be as good as those purchased individually.
- We have compared this to buying a box of candy and finding that you only like caramels. Nonetheless, a nice gift.

ALTERNATIVES:

Buy individual products in the quantities you need.

PADDING AND COVERING DEVICES

TYPES AVAILABLE:

- ☐ Corner guards
- ☐ Edge guards
- ☐ Doorknob covers
- ☐ Faucet guards
- ☐ Tub pads

INTENDED FUNCTION:

To shield sharp areas so that if a child falls against them, the blow will be softened.

☐ Corner guards are simple plastic caps that attach to the corners of desks and tables.

☐ Edge-guard material comes in rolls of clear plastic and attaches to straight edges of tables and countertops that appear unsafe.

☐ Doorknob covers prevent children from turning doorknobs and entering rooms you wish to keep off limits. A parent can operate them easily by grasping the covered doorknob firmly, applying pressure, and turning knob.

☐ Faucet guards are used to cushion the bathtub faucet areas. They are usually made of a dense foam product. There is also an inflatable version.

☐ Tub pads prevent a baby from slipping in the tub during the first year.

HOW TO INSTALL:

☐ Corner and edge guards: Generally they come packaged with accompanying adhesive strips. The adhesive is affixed first and the corner or edge guard over that. Make sure the sharp surface is clean before putting down the adhesive.

☐ Doorknob covers: Simply slide over the doorknobs. One plastic version comes in two pieces: when the two-piece model snaps together over the doorknob it resembles the one-piece model.

☐ Faucet guards and tub pads: Simply fit in place.

SHORTCOMINGS:

☐ Corner guards:

- They are often difficult to fit, since all furniture corners are not perfectly angular. You may need to try several brands before you are satisfied with the fit.
- The adhesive eventually wears out.
- Most are small enough to be considered a choking hazard.
- They will not adhere well to an unclean surface.

☐ Edge guards:

- Because edge guards are packaged in a roll, they have a tendency to stay coiled and never quite straighten out enough to be secured effectively to the edge, especially if you purchase an older package (check for yellowing of strip).
- The adhesive wears out.
- The edges must be angular for the edge guard to adhere properly.
- Because the plastic is not soft, the guards only prevent skin breaking in the event of a fall; it will still hurt.
- If one section comes loose, a child may well tug at it and the whole thing will come off.
- Suction-cup designs are unreliable.

☐ Doorknob covers:

Plastic

- The little round grippers on either side have a tendency to fall off, which makes it difficult to grasp the doorknob effectively. The grippers are also a choking hazard.
- In the two-piece version, installation can often be awkward and frequent removal and reinstallation can cause breakage.
- Odd-shaped doorknobs cannot accommodate these covers.
- They are annoying to visitors.
- They can pinch!

Puffy

- They are easily removed once a child figures out how to do it.
- They are not well suited for doors leading outside.

☐ Faucet guards:

- The inflatable version may be punctured.
- They are mold collectors.
- Some models are made of poor-quality foam that may not be resistant enough to prevent a serious blow.

☐ Tub pads:

- Not a necessity.
- Tend to be pulled off by curious children.

Doorknob covers

a. standard plastic

b. two-piece

c. soft

Doorknob covers are used to prevent entry into off-limits rooms. Designed to fit loosely but securely over a doorknob, they spin around when a small child attempts to turn the knob.

ALTERNATIVES:

☐ Corners, edges and the like:

- Use some thick foam and strong adhesive tape to pad the corners.
- If the piece of furniture in question has extremely sharp corners—for example, some glass-topped tables—remove the piece.
- Cut a cross design in an old tennis ball and place it over the sharp corner. This temporary pad works

well on fireplace hearths and other awkward corners.

☐ Doorknob covers:

- A plain circle of cloth attached to the doorknob with a rubber band will sometimes work.
- Install a hook-and-eye latch or flip lock high up on the door frame.

LATCHES AND CLOSURES

TYPES AVAILABLE:

☐ Drawer and cabinet latches

☐ Velcro latches

☐ U-bar closures

☐ Window latches

☐ Refrigerator/appliance latches

☐ Toilet latches

☐ Door latches

INTENDED FUNCTION:

To prevent children from opening drawers, cupboards, cabinets, appliances, toilet lids, and doors. Window latches are specifically designed to prevent falls.

HOW TO INSTALL:

☐ Drawer, cabinet, window, and door latches that include screws; carefully follow package instructions and mark drill holes. When installing latches on hardwood cabinet doors, carefully choose the appropriate drill bit and drill about 1/4 inch deep at your markings. Screw in the device, making any slight adjustments before tightening. Often latches can be installed without a drill.

PADDING AND COVERING DEVICES

TYPE	MANUFACTURER	AVG. PRICE	RATING	COMMENTS
Corner Guards Ikea Patrull	Ikea, Inc. Plymouth Commons Plymouth Meeting, PA 19462	$1.50	★★★	Large, white, easy to install
Bumpers	Belwith International Kiddie Guard P.O. Box 6954 City of Industry, CA 91748	$2	★★	Small brown covers.
Corner Cushions	KinderGard 14822 Venture Drive Dallas, TX 75234	$2	★★	Clear and small.
Edge Guards Edge Cushion	KinderGard 14822 Venture Drive Dallas, TX 75234	$5 up	★★	Difficult to install. Try to move the dangerous object rather than edging around it. Can be pulled off by curious toddler.

Doorknob Covers				
Plastic Knob Covers	Baby World Co., Inc. Station Plaza East Great Neck, NY 11021	$1.50 up	★★★	Easy to install. Children eventually learn how to pull these off and can open the door.
Doorknob Guards	KinderGard 14822 Venture Drive Dallas, TX 75234	$2.50 up	★★	Two-piece installation. Frustrating for visitors and parents. Short life span.
KinderKraft Doorknob Cover	KinderKraft 501 N. Jefferson St. Arlington, VA 22205	$3	★★	Soft, puffy, handcrafted. Short life span.
Tub Pads				
Bathtub Sponges	Pansey Ellen Products 7025-a Amwiler Industrial Park Atlanta, GA 30360	$5 up	★★★	Slip-resistant surface for your child to sit on while bathing. Also can be used to cushion a high chair.

TYPE	MANUFACTURER	AVG. PRICE	RATING	COMMENTS
Faucet Guards Safety Bear	Family Life Products Box 541 Dennis, MA 02638	$7.50 up	★★★	Bathtub spot cover. Worthwhile investment. Long life, easy to clean. Similar products are manufactured by several other companies.
Faucet Friends	A-Plus Products, Inc. Box 2975 Beverly Hills, CA 90213	$15	★★★★	Covers the entire spout and faucet area. Must be removed to adjust water flow.
Inflatable Soft Spout	Safety 1st 200 Boylston St. Chestnut Hill, MA 02167	$1.99 up	★★	Inflatable bathtub spout cover. Has a weak spot near seam. May not last long. Easy to travel with.

RATING SCALE KEY — ★★★★ excellent ★★★ good ★★ average ★ poor

☐ Velcro latches: One side of the Velcro strip is affixed to, for example, the stereo lid, and the other to the stereo base. This should prevent little hands from lifting the lid and having it fall on their fingers. Using isopropyl alcohol, make sure all surfaces are clean before affixing adhesive.

☐ U-bar closures: Detach the closing piece by pushing in one or both squeeze buttons. When the closing piece is loosened, the U-piece can be slipped through two handles or over two knobs on a cabinet door. Tighten the closing piece to secure the device in place.

☐ Refrigerator and appliance latches: Measure carefully and clean the surface of the appliance first. Peel off seal and adhere adhesive to the dry surface.

☐ Toilet latch: Read instructions carefully, since models tend to vary. Avoid adhesives and Velcro devices.

SHORTCOMINGS:

☐ Drawer and cabinet latches:

- Not all latches work on all cabinets (see illustration).
- Leftover drill holes when your baby grows up.
- Some brands are made of poor-quality plastic and will break easily.
- It is difficult to know ahead of time which brand's design is best suited to your home. Long shaft? Button? Two-pronged design? You may need to try several brands before you are satisfied.
- At a certain developmental stage, your child will be able to undo any latch. Therefore, a latch is not a replacement for a lock and key with close supervision.

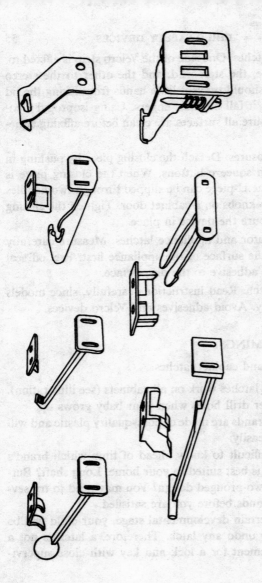

Latches

Latches differ dramatically in size, durability, ease of installation, and effectiveness. Shop carefully before choosing a latch for your cabinets.

☐ Velcro latches:

- The adhesive will not adhere well on dirty, dusty, greasy, or painted surfaces.
- Children love to play with Velcro. It becomes an attraction rather than a deterrent.
- The size of the Velcro strip is not always suitable.

☐ U-bar closures: Some brands malfunction on a regular basis.

☐ Window latches: Windows cannot be opened for full ventilation unless some form of window grate is installed.

☐ Refrigerator/appliance latches:

- Most appliance doors have a tight seal and are too heavy for toddlers to open. Any toddler who can open these doors can quickly outsmart these devices. Adhesive latches have a short life-span.
- May take off some paint when the appliance latch is removed.

☐ Toilet latches:

- Anyone using the toilet must remember to flip or attach the lid closure over the top of the lid after each use. New habits are not always easy to develop.
- Visitors may not know how to relatch.
- Children learn quickly; the device has a short life-span.

☐ Door latches:

- The effectiveness of the latch depends on how careful adults are after opening the door. Supervision and the habit of relatching after each use will maintain a high level of safety.

Toilet Latch

The toilet poses a hazard during a brief period in your child's development. A latch like the one pictured can help provide security.

ALTERNATIVES:
☐ Drawers and cabinets:
- Move all breakables and toxins from low shelves to high shelves. Make all the cabinets safe for children.
- Use a ribbon or elastic to secure the knobs or handles shut.
- Remove handles. This won't always work, depending on the design of the handle and cabinet or drawer. Try removing handles on the china cabinet or those drawers that are rarely used.
- Most contemporary drawers have built-in safety

catches to prevent drawers from pulling out and falling. A short screw or nail on the back of a drawer can serve the same purpose as a drawer catch.

☐ Windows:

- Keep windows latched or locked at all times.
- Make sure windows are out of reach, with tight screens.

☐ Refrigerator/appliances:

- Block entrance to the kitchen using a door or gate if it poses too many hazards.

☐ Toilet latch:

- Use a doorknob cover or hook-and-eye latch on bathroom door.
- Maintain close supervision when your baby is in the bathroom. Remember, many toilet drownings occur while visiting someone else's home.

☐ Door latches: A doorknob cover or alarm may be simpler.

LATCHES AND CLOSURES

TYPE	MANUFACTURER	AVG. PRICE	RATING	COMMENTS
Drawer and Cabinet *Screw-In* Push-button	Gerber Products Co. 445 State St. Fremont, MI 49412	$3.50	★ ★	Works on drawers and cabinets. 1-piece, 2-screw design. Toddlers can unlatch before long.
Safe'Lok	Mericom Corporation 8562 Canton Center Rd. Canton, MI 48187	$1.50	★ ★ ★	Trap-slot design. 2-piece, 4-screw installation. Prevents cabinet from reclosing on a child's fingers.
KinderGard	KinderGard 14822 Venture Dr. Dallas, TX 75234	$3.50	★ ★ ★	Classic hook-catch design. Du Pont formula plastic. 4-screw installation with an average-length shaft.

Baby Guards	Playskool Baby Hasbro Inc. 108 Fairway Ct. Northvale, NJ 07647	$1.50	★★	V-shaped slot, 2-piece, 4-screw installation.
Superlatch	Baby's Dream, Inc. P.O. Box 1234 Miami, FL 33126	$3	★★	Most expensive variety. Complicated design and installation. 4-in-1 multipurpose latch. Du Pont formula plastic resists strain over 264 pounds. Long shaft fits most cabinets and drawers.
Child Safety Latch	Shur-Lok Manufacturing Co. 413 North Main St. Hutchins, TX 75141	$2	★★	2-piece, 4-screw installation.
3 Safety Latches	The First Years One Kiddie Dr. Avon, MA 02322	$2	★★	1-piece metal design with 3-screw installation. Guaranteed.

RATING SCALE KEY ★★★★ excellent ★★★ good ★★ average ★ poor

TYPE	MANUFACTURER	AVG. PRICE	RATING	COMMENTS
Safety Door	Sanitoy, Inc. Nursery Needs Nursery Lane P.O. Box 2167 Fitchburg, MA 01420	$2	★★	2-prong, 2-piece design. 4-screw installation. Difficult to align and install. Warranty. Plastic prongs eventually bend, misaligning the latch. Works on most contemporary drawers.
Adhesives Button Latch	Baby World Co. P.O. Box 219 Grafton, WV 26354	$1	★★	Designed to work on medicine chests although not recommended to child-proof toxins. Clean area first and use extra glue to assure a longer life span.

Lock and Key Design				
Ikea Patrull	Ikea Inc. Plymouth Commons Plymouth Meeting, PA 19462	$3.50	★★★	Comes with proper drill bit to assure a neat installation. Fits most drawers and cabinets although directions are poor.
Velcro Latches				
Auto Safety	Numerous manufacturers	$2.50	★	Assures that button latch on car seat belt cannot be easily unbuckled.
Garbage Gard Fastening System	Velcro USA Inc. 406 Brown Ave. Manchester, NH 03108	$2.50	★	Clean and dry all surfaces first, using isopropyl alcohol. Best choice among Velcro products.

RATING SCALE KEY ★★★★ excellent ★★★ good ★★ average ★ poor

TYPE	MANUFACTURER	AVG. PRICE	RATING	COMMENTS
Velcro Safety Strap	Growtime Cutoy Cooperative Assoc. P.O. Box 22057 Los Angeles, CA 90022	$2.50	★	Self-sticking latch. Clean and dry all surfaces. Do not use on high-risk areas such as toilet lids. Guaranteed.
U-Bars (closed-end)	KinderGard Corp. 14822 Venture Dr. Dallas, TX 75234	$1.50 up	★★★	Do not use to child-proof toxins. Most brands are easy to use on knobs or handles.
Window Latches	Ikea Inc. Plymouth Commons Plymouth Meeting, PA 19462	$1.50 up	★★★	Check your local hardware store for latches and window grates.
Door Latches	Child Safe Inc. 333 Camino Gardens Blvd.-F Boca Raton, FL 33432	$1 up	★	Check your local hardware store for hook-and-eye latches and other flip-latch designs. Avoid cheap plastics.

Refrigerator and Appliance Latches Playskool Baby Guards	Playskool Baby Hasbro, Inc. 108 Fairway Ct. Northvale, NJ 07647	$2 up	★★	Usually not necessary. Adhesives have a short life span. Adhere with additional cement product if you want it to last.
Toilet Lid Latches Lid Lok	Mericom 8562 Canton Center Rd. Canton, MI 48187	$7	★★★	Made of Noryl, chemical-resistant plastic. No adhesives, easy installation.
Playskool Baby Guards	Playskool Baby Hasbro, Inc. 108 Fairway Ct. Northvale, NJ 07647	$3	★	Adhesive latch design provides for a short functional time. Does not fit on all toilet seats.

RATING SCALE KEY ★★★★ excellent ★★★ good ★★ average ★ poor

MISCELLANEOUS SAFETY DEVICES

There are a great many safety products that do not fall under any particular category. Among them, the more popular are:

- Fingerprinting kits and information bracelets.
- Car safety accessories
- Thermometers (for use in testing bottles and bath water)
- Stickers, decals, and signs
- Videotapes on child safety
- Tub seating devices
- Medicine safes and kits
- Fire escape ladders
- Stove protectors and stove knob guards
- Whistles
- Miscellaneous safety hardware
- Shoelace tie-ups
- Bed guards
- Emergency information boards to post near telephone
- Glass door safety film for sliding glass doors
- Anti-slip underlays and carpet tapes
- Door-slamming protectors

Most of these devices appeal directly to a parent's guilt. The child safety product business would have you believe that these items are essential to your child's well-being. What's more, new items are released on the market virtually every week making it difficult to keep up with all the products available. We are here to say, be selective. Choose the devices you wish to install carefully, and when you shop for them compare the different brands available. Above all, do not be fooled into thinking these items will make very much difference.

Some safety devices are definitely worth the investment of money, time, and energy. But remember, nothing can substitute for a little rearranging and close parental attention.

MISCELLANEOUS SAFETY DEVICES

TYPE	MANUFACTURER	AVG. PRICE	RATING	COMMENTS
Fingerprint Kits and Child Information Bracelets				
TravAlert Child Information Bracelet	Safety 1st 200 Boylston St. Chestnut Hill, MA 02167	$3.50 up	★★	Simple wristband design. Useful for 3-year-olds on up for vacations and tours, amusement parks, crowded events. A toddler most likely would discard the device.
Fingerprint Kits	Numerous manufacturers	$5 up	★	Choose an inkless variety. Better yet, have the professionals do it for you free of charge. Contact your local police or sheriff's office.

Miscellaneous Car Safety Accessories			
Head Guard Safety Cushions	Intermark, Inc. The Safe Sit Co. 4379 Wilshire Blvd. Mound, MN 55364	$7 up	★★★	Makes traveling more comfortable for newborns. Can also be used on swings and strollers.
Back-seat Rearview Mirrors	Children on the Go Wheeling, IL 60090 Childsafe Products 2509 E. Thousand Oaks Blvd. Suite 401 Thousand Oaks, CA 91360	$7 up	★★	A bit distracting. Not a necessity, but certainly a reassuring view for new parents. Encourages adults to keep car seats in the safest area of the car, the back seat.
Locking Clips	Century Products, Inc. Gerber Products Co. 1366 Commerce Dr. Stow, OH 44224	$2	★★★	Used to keep seat belts from automatically retracting. Useful for proper installation of most car seats.

RATING SCALE KEY ★★★★ excellent ★★★ good ★★ average ★ poor

TYPE	MANUFACTURER	AVG. PRICE	RATING	COMMENTS
Car Shades (stick-on, suction, pull shades, umbrellas)	Prince Lionheart 2301 Cape Cod Way Santa Ana, CA 92730	$5 up	★★★	Avoid any model that interferes with the driver's vision. All shades arranged within a toddler's reach can easily be torn down. The least expensive vinyl models are the most practical choice.
Car Seat Shield Covers	Nanci Industries P.O. Box 241 Germantown, MD 20874	$10 up	★★	Custom car-seat cover that slides over metal bars and pads. Machine washable. Fits only limited car-seat designs. As an alternative, try wrapping masking tape around metal frame.
Thermometers (bottle, bath, forehead)	Clinitemp Inc. P.O. Box 40273 Indianapolis, IN 46240	$2	★★	These devices can assist a first-time parent. They do not detect hot spots in fluids.

Stickers, Decals, and Signs			
Tot Spotter Fire Rescue Decals	Safety 1st 200 Boylston St. Chestnut Hills, MA 02167	$2	★★	Firefighters enter a burning house low to the ground. It makes sense to post these stickers on the lower half of a bedroom door rather than in public view on a bedroom window.
Reflective Tape	Kenyon Consumer 200 Main Street Kenyon, RI 02836	$1 up	★★★	Useful on bike clothing and helmets, Halloween costumes, tricycles and wagons.
Mr. "No" Poison Safety Decals	Safety 1st 200 Boylston St. Chestnut Hills, MA 02167	$1.50 up	★★★	Free poison stickers are also available from regional poison-control centers (see Appendix 3)

RATING SCALE KEY ★★★★ excellent ★★★ good ★★ average ★ poor

TYPE	MANUFACTURER	AVG. PRICE	RATING	COMMENTS
"Baby on Board" suction-cup car signs	Safety 1st 200 Boylston St. Chestnut Hills, MA 02167	$2.50	★★	
Videotapes "David Horowitz Presents: The Baby-Safe Home"	McGraw-Hill Book Company 1221 Avenue of the Americas New York, NY 10020	$19	★★	Unfortunately outdated demonstration of rescuing a choking child.
Tub Seating Devices Bath Ring	A-Plus Products P.O. Box 2975 Beverly Hills, CA 90213	$10 up	★★	Designs have improved since early models first appeared. This can tempt parents to let down their guard. Children often do not fit into the ring. Suction cups do not stick well unless tub is clean and free of soap film.

Medicine Safes and Kits			
Medi-Safe	Inter-continental Marketing Systems 10600 Mastin Overland Park, KS 66212	$10	★★★★	Perfect for travel and convenient to use at bedside or on countertop. 30-day warranty.
The Kids Care Kit	The Cherubs Collection 1462 Pegaso St. Encinitas, CA 92024	$15	★★	Complete first-aid kit designed for concerned parents. Alternative is to compile your own tailored first-aid kit.
Safe-T-First	H. G. Arms Co. 1449 37th St. Brooklyn, NY 11218	$18	★★	Security cabinet that fits into all standard medicine cabinets. Includes lock and 2 keys.
Fire Escape Ladders	Numerous manufacturers	$30–150	★★	Second- and third-story lengths. Keep in closet while children are young.

RATING SCALE KEY ★★★★ excellent ★★★ good ★★ average ★ poor

TYPE	MANUFACTURER	AVG. PRICE	RATING	COMMENTS
Stove Protectors Range Top Guard	GW DMKA, Inc. 196 Van Winkle Ave. Garfield, NJ 07628	$20	★	Adjustable, but does not necessarily keep tempting stove knobs out of reach. Fingers can still poke through to a hot burner. Suction cups loosen with stove grease.
Kelshannon Stove/ Oven Shield	Kelshannon Development Corp. 179 B. Washington Ave. Dumont, NJ 07628	$40	★	This clear shield is secured with adhesives which have a short life span. It would be more economical to gate your kitchen. Children tend to drop toys over the top of this guard, making it an attraction.

Playskool Baby Guards Stove Knob Covers	Playskool Baby Hasbro, Inc. 108 Fairway Ct. Northvale, NJ 07647	$9	★	Designed to spin around stove knobs when small children reach to turn them. Bothersome for the cook and expensive. If stove knobs are a problem, take them off and use them only when you're cooking.
Whistles Zip and Clip Whistles	F. J. Straco Co. 1107 Broadway New York, NY 10010	$1.50 up	★★★	Teaching children to blow a whistle for help is an old idea now marketed with a new look. Choo-choo train, truck, teddy bear, and heart designs.
Bed Guards King-size Bed Rail 60" long	Cosco Products 2525 State St. Columbia, IN 47201	$14	★★	A mattress on the floor serves the same function.

RATING SCALE KEY ★★★★ excellent ★★★ good ★★ average ★ poor

TYPE	MANUFACTURER	AVG. PRICE	RATING	COMMENTS
Emergency Information Boards				
Sitter Safety Cards and Information Boards	Numerous manufacturers	$1.50 up	★★	Some versions allow additional important information. Make your own emergency phone list.
Miscellaneous Safety Hardware				
Toy chest or box lid supports	Brainerd Mfg. Co. P.O. Box 3667 East Rochester, NY 14445	$3 up	★★	Available to install on chests that do not already have a proper hinge device.
Shoelace tie-up devices	Numerous manufacturers	$2 up	★	Buy Velcro-strapped shoes if loose ties are a problem. Some versions have bells to signal that your child is wandering away.

Product	Rating	Price	Manufacturer	Description
Anti-slip underlays and carpet tape for throw rugs	★★★	$5–25	Numerous manufacturers	Worthwhile investment for any loose carpets in your home.
Glass Door Safety Film Clean Window	★★	$30	Lillian Vernon 510 S. Fulton Ave. Mount Vernon, NY 10550	A clear adhesive window film. Tricky installation. A tinted version would be helpful for small children.
Door Slamming Protectors Playskool Baby Guards Slam Guard	★	$5	Playskool Baby Hasbro, Inc. 108 Fairway Ct. Northvale, NJ 07628	Designed to allow a gap between door and frame to avoid pinched fingers. When the door swings shut, the device is designed to slow down the motion. Unreliable. A possible choice for child-proofing swinging doors.

RATING SCALE KEY ★★★★ excellent ★★★ good ★★ average ★ poor

Chapter Three

Hazards Found Throughout the House

Now that you know about the many devices available, you may well be curious as to where these devices may prove most useful. Why not begin by taking a closer look at each room in your house?

Imagine that you are touring it for the first time. Keep in mind, this will be no ordinary tour. It will require a little imaginative research on your part. Your view and vision of your house are not going to provide you with all the information necessary to recognize the myriad potential dangers to your child. You will need to expand on what you know as an adult and go a step beyond. You need to look at your house the way your child sees it. Only from this unique vantage point will you become aware of the house your child lives in and the obstacles that it contains for her. Merely walking through and trying to think like a small child is not enough. You have got to move like one.

So parents, drop down to your hands and knees and start exploring your house. You will be amazed at what you discover about your child's perceptions, enticements, and frustrations. There is so much more to every room than what you see from "up here." Every corner, piece of furniture, window, and doorway takes on a different light, depth, position. This is the house you need to child-proof. When you have successfully completed this exercise, you will be ready for your upright tour.

Once you have experienced your house by tot's eye view, you will realize what you are up against. The task of child-proofing may seem monumental—unmanageable, even. But fear not. The actual task of physically childproofing your house is not time-consuming once you have decided exactly what changes need to be made and purchased the supplies you may need. Your best bet for success is to get organized. That is what this chapter and the next one can help you do.

What follows is a list of those childproofing concerns common to many rooms in your home. Chapter Four will be dedicated to outlining those concerns peculiar to specific rooms. Take the time to secure your home now so that you and that lovable bundle of trouble can enjoy this magic time in relative peace and mutual discovery.

So, walk through your rooms with us and start making a list of the changes you feel are necessary. We've included a list at the very end of this book to help you keep track of the items you may wish to purchase, and the quantities needed of each item. Easier to set the kid down in the playpen you say? Maybe. But we know you will have much more fun making your house that safe place where you and your child can play and enjoy the adventure together.

ELECTRICAL HAZARDS

☐ Install plastic caps in empty electrical outlets that cannot be blocked by heavy furniture. Caution: caps are a choking hazard, so make sure they fit snugly. Consider installing an electrical outlet cover over the plugs you frequently use for vacuuming or for other appliances used occasionally.

☐ Install permanent covers over electrical outlets that have engaged plugs (lamps, TVs, clocks). The cover will keep children from tugging on cords or tucking small fingers into an electrical connection.

☐ Check electrical cords for fraying or apparent damage. Discard or repair items with unsafe wiring.

☐ Check the electrical box. Latch it if it is within reach of a curious toddler.

☐ Avoid using grounded adapters that convert a three-prong plug into a two-prong one. (Look for the grounded ones that have a floating wire.)

☐ Avoid extension cords. If you must use them, try sealing the union between the two cords with electrical tape (plastic tape will do). If no tape is available, cap any electrical openings that a child might suck, bite, or poke something into.

☐ Use the proper extension cord. Do not plug a three-prong plug into a two-prong cord.

☐ Never leave an extension cord electrically engaged at one end and open on the opposite end.

☐ Avoid using old, brittle extension cords.

☐ Make sure, both at home and away, that there are no loose metal objects lying around that can be inserted into outlets. Such items include knives, keys, scissors, screwdrivers, bobby pins, wire, safety pins, or nails. Keeping wastebaskets out of reach is a must.

☐ Check all light bulbs. They should be firmly in place. Never leave a socket empty.

☐ Never use a larger-sized fuse to replace one of a lower amp. Know the electrical capacity of your home and refrain from using too many appliances at one time, which can cause an overload or possible fire.

☐ Keep electrical fans up and out of reach. Consider a ceiling fan as an alternative.

☐ Have an electrician install GFCI (ground fault circuit interrupters) in any location where water and electricity are near each other—bathrooms, outdoors, pool and fountain areas, kitchen sink area, basement, and all major appliances. The GFCI will sense an electrical fault and immediately break the circuit below a danger level.

☐ Tie up slack and tape down any electrical or telephone cords. Consider using a plastic cord shortener for a neat arrangement in areas where the cords are not blocked by furniture.

☐ Avoid "octopus" connections where many electrical cords are adapted to fit into one wall outlet.

HEAT SOURCES AND FIRE HAZARDS

☐ Plan fire escape routes. Consider storing a safety ladder for exiting a multistoried house.

☐ Use only book matches in your home. They are more difficult for small children to strike.

☐ If you buy a fire extinguisher for your home, choose a multipurpose, dry chemical unit. Mount fire extinguishers in a convenient location but out of a child's reach.

☐ Set your water heater at 120 degrees F. A plumber or utility company representative can make this adjustment for you. There are ways to install dual-control pipes for

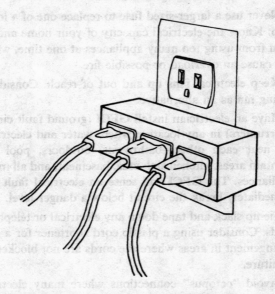

Octopus connections are a hazard for two reasons: they can easily overload your circuits, and they cannot be adequately child-proofed.

very hot water to run into washers if you are concerned about cleanliness.

☐ Remember that aerosol products are very explosive and should be disposed of safely. Never puncture them or throw them into the fireplace.

☐ Cigarette butts are a burn hazard and a choking hazard, and many are toxic. Remember to keep ashtrays clean and up high.

☐ Avoid space heaters. If fuel-burning heaters are used, make sure the area is well ventilated.

☐ Any hot radiators should be childproofed with a barricade.

FLOORS

☐ Repair or replace any splintered, cracked or torn linoleum floors.

☐ Keep floors picked up to prevent any trips and falls. Never stack junk on or at the bottom of the stairs!

☐ Floors need to be kept free of oil, grease, water, or juice, and slick wax surfaces.

☐ Secure area rugs or carpets that slide or curl. You can upgrade carpet padding or add a layer of anti-slip material, use double-sided carpet tape, or secure carpet or rug to the floor with carpet tacks. (Have a carpet professional help you do this properly.)

FURNITURE

☐ Try capping the bottom of chair legs that slide easily. You will find rubber caps of assorted sizes at your local hardware store.

☐ Remove or secure any furniture, artwork, floor lamps, or other equipment that could cause a child to trip.

☐ Cap or tape foam over any sharp corners or edges of your furniture.

☐ Keep your decorating simple for the first three years of your child's life. Remove any obviously hazardous furniture (glass coffee tables, extra lamps, sharp-cornered tables and chairs).

☐ Check desks and drawers for any potential hazard. If the drawers pull out easily, hammer a small nail or two along the back edge as a catch. This should help prevent it from falling completely out. Commercial drawer-stopping devices are also available.

LIGHTING

☐ Hallways should be well lit. We suggest the use of dimmer switches rather than novelty night lights for safe nighttime navigation.

☐ Maintain adequate lighting in your home to help prevent falls. Have light switches available within reach. Avoid having to journey through a dark room just to turn a light on.

BALCONIES

Avoid them if possible! If you must, ask yourself these questions and make a firm commitment to keep the door locked and out of use for the next few years.

☐ Is there any open railing? Are spaces more than 4 inches in between?

☐ Is the railing or wall secure?

☐ Is there any way that a child could climb up and over by standing on furniture or stacked toys?

WINDOWS

Window accidents frequently occur when kids climb furniture to see what is going on outside. Even window screens cannot withstand the weight of a leaning child.

When screens are pushed out, there is nothing left to prevent a child from falling out the window.

☐ Avoid placing furniture underneath windows. Install devices that allow the window to be opened only slightly. Since windows are designed differently, consult your hardware dealer for the locking device that will solve your problem. Another alternative is to install window grates. These are also available in many large hardware stores.

☐ Test all of your windows. Make sure they are screened. Check to see if the screen pushes out easily. If your window appears to be a risk, you can: install window gates or safety railings; install a window childproofing device allowing partial opening of windows; keep windows closed and inform houseguests of the risk (do not hesitate to ask for their cooperation).

☐ For advice on window cords see Choking and Suffocation Hazards.

STAIRWAYS

☐ Set the rules early and teach children in their first year the proper behavior around stairways. Teach infants how to negotiate down stairs on their tummies, feet first. Older children should know not to roughhouse or carry large items that block their vision on the stairs.

☐ Never leave piles of clutter on steps.

☐ No loose throw rugs at the top of the stairway.

☐ Lighting should be adequate with switches at both the top and bottom of the stairway.

☐ Stair surface should provide adequate traction with rubber treads, carpeting, or nonslip paint.

☐ If your home has a particularly hazardous top or bottom step, consider highlighting it with a strip of fluorescent tape.

☐ Check to make sure stairs and railings are in good repair. Give railings a good shake.

☐ Spacing in between balusters should be no more than 4 inches. If the gap is too large, consider having your handyman install a Lucite barricade along the railing. Another option is to keep stairways gated during the early years.

☐ Check location of furniture. There should be no climbable furniture near a staircase.

☐ When babies are still quite small, gate the top of your stairways. As soon as your child is able to crawl away from you, gate the bottom of the stairway (up two or three steps to allow some exploration is in most cases an acceptable option).

☐ If you have a door leading down to a basement, consider gating the stairs anyway. Often, a habit of closing the door will slip and a toddler or small baby in a walker will tumble down.

DOORS

STANDARD DOORS

☐ Make absolutely sure that no doors in your house lock from the inside without access from another entrance or with a key. A child can easily get stuck inside, creating a frantic situation for everyone. If this hazard does exist you have several options:

- Change the lock
- Remove the doorknob altogether
- Latch the door and discuss an emergency plan in case someone does get locked inside
- A short-term remedy is to try slinging a towel over the top of the door to keep it from closing.

☐ Swinging doors are a difficult problem. We suggest that you latch the door in an open position using a simple hook-and-eye device. If the door is useful in keeping your child out of an off-limits area, purchase a gate rather than dealing with the swinging door.

☐ Hydraulic closures on storm doors or screen doors can prevent both pinched fingers and slamming doors.

☐ Consider using a knob cover to keep small children out of hazardous rooms. But keep in mind that this device will not last forever and is not a guarantee.

STORM DOORS, GLASS DOORS AND WALLS

Tempered safety glass is the premium choice for safety. Laminated or wired safety glass and Lucite panels are less expensive choices. For existing glass there are still measures you can take to avoid accidents:

☐ Keep screen doors shut.

☐ Use stickers, decals, or your child's artwork posted at tot's eye level (adult's eye level too) to show the glass door is closed.

☐ Position furniture strategically.

☐ Establish the "No Running" rule early!

TRASH CONTROL

☐ Try limiting trash to the kitchen and bathrooms.

☐ Keep trash out of reach by using latches if necessary. However, devices will not provide a perfect solution so you need backup childproofing as well. We have found that the safest alternative is to locate the can under the sink with a latched cabinet door.

☐ Try to keep safety in mind when you throw out your trash. For instance, tuck sharp cans and plastic bags (tied in knots) down at the bottom of your garbage can. Habits like this provide an extra margin of safety.

☐ If you line trash cans, use paper or "crinkly" plastic bags (the kind used by most department stores). No thin, clingy plastic liners.

CHOKING AND SUFFOCATION HAZARDS

☐ Lock or latch anything your child can crawl into and become stranded. Consider drilling ventilation holes in any hazards of this kind just in case.

☐ Remove all trunks and footlockers that do not have spring-loaded hinges and ventilation holes.

☐ Remove any plastic bags—especially dry-cleaning bags and trash-can liners.

☐ Scan for hanging cords or strings of any sort longer than 12 inches.

☐ Dangling phone cords can be a problem. Suggestions:

- Get in the habit of wrapping the cord around the phone after each use.

- Screw a cup hook into the wall to hang the cord on after each use.
- Buy a cordless remote phone to use for a few years.
- Place the phone up high out of reach.

☐ Window cords found on curtains or venetian blinds are a primary concern. The following tips may help:

- When buying curtains or blinds, specify in advance that you would prefer short cords or plastic sticks.
- If you have curtains that run cords through a pulley attached to the floor, you can either dismantle cords and tie up and out of reach or tape cords together so children cannot become entangled in them.
- Cut, tape, or untie all loops.
- Never place a crib, portable crib or bassinet near a window with hanging cords.
- Secure all cords out of reach.
- Wrap the cord around itself or use a long twist tie to secure it.
- Cleats can easily be mounted to wind the window cord securely up high and out of reach.
- Toss the cord up and over the curtain rod.

CLOSETS

☐ We have found the thin plastic covering on dry cleaning the most outstanding hazard in a new parent's closet. Remove this covering and tie it in knots as soon as you bring it home. Dispose of it by tucking it at the bottom of your trash can. Consider the location of your child's car seat and locate the dry cleaning safely away from it when driving home.

☐ Check behind clothes and boxes for exposed electrical outlets. Cap or cover open outlets.

☐ Remove any mothballs.

☐ Check door locks. Consider a hook and eye located high on the outside of the closet door to keep small children out. Another option: Try a doorknob cover for a few years.

☐ Evaluate the contents of your closet. Check for falling hazards such as vacuum cleaners, ironing boards, and brooms. Check for poisons, hazardous trunks, and small items a toddler could choke on, such as loose change or buttons.

☐ Check the light fixture; a hanging fixture with a dangling chain or a long string can pose a threat.

POISONING HAZARDS

It may be a good idea to carry an empty box with you on your room-by-room tour. You will find yourself gathering toxins from more than one room in your house.

☐ House plants are a common poison that we often thoughtlessly expose children to. Using Appendix 1 as a reference, check your house plants for toxicity. If you are uncertain, take a leaf to a florist or nursery and find out. Locate poisonous plants out of reach or live without them for a few years.

☐ On all gas utilities:

- Remove handles and store out of reach, or
- Place a shield over the gas knobs, or
- Disconnect unused gas fixtures and seal off the gas source. If you ever smell gas, open the windows and call the gas company for help.

☐ Lead-based paint is still a problem. If you live in an older house it is very likely that layers of lead-based paint line your walls or the exterior of your house. Ingestion of peeling paint is your primary concern. You should:

- Renovate areas posing obvious dangers, such as bubbled, cracked, or chipped paint. Strip off old paint and use wallpaper, paneling, or ceiling tiles to cover these areas.
- Monitor playtime and keep children from chewing on windowsills or old furniture, picking paint chips, or playing in any area where paint and plaster dust could have fallen.

☐ Do not burn colored newsprint or magazines in your fireplace.

☐ If you have pipes more than fifty years old or live in a neighborhood that may have old pipes, have your water analyzed to check for lead and other toxic chemicals.

☐ Set an example: avoid taking medicines and vitamins in front of your little ones. Refrain from calling them "candy."

☐ Check household pens. Know whether they are toxic or nontoxic. Store the toxic pens with other household poisons and throw out anything that is questionable.

☐ Try buying medicines in small sample bottles. A child who has swallowed three tablets is far better off than a child who has swallowed fifty! Beware, though: many samplers do not have child-resistant packaging.

☐ Lock up any toxic products. Locks are more reliable than a plastic latch. More than one eighteen-month-old has unlatched a childproof cabinet.

☐ Use three-tiered hanging baskets to store mildly toxic but frequently used materials out of reach. Nursery changing table items like creams, disinfectant sprays, and baby powder fall into this category. Remember, though, a climber can get into anything!

☐ Put poison control stickers (with the poison control center's hotline number) on all toxins. Teach "danger" and associate it with the stickers. See Appendix 3 for information on locating your nearest poison control center and obtaining stickers.

☐ Have poison antidotes on hand: Syrup of Ipecac may be advised by your poison center to induce vomiting, and activated charcoal may be advised to neutralize a petroleum-based poison. Know where these items are stored and make sure the information is posted for sitters.

☐ Make sure child-resistant closures are on all your medicines. Do not drop your guard, though. Many toddlers can bite off these caps and eat the contents or feed them to a younger child.

☐ Keep all harmful products in their original bottle or can and make sure they are well labeled. Never store toxins in food containers.

☐ Dispose of old medicines by flushing them down the toilet before discarding the bottle.

☐ When we are not feeling well it is difficult to stay with our safety routine. We may find ourselves taking chances by leaving medicines on countertops or the bathroom sink. By planning ahead, we can avoid these problems.

- Small "Medi-safe" lockable boxes are available to hold a few medicines. Perfect for a temporary bedside infirmary. Take one to the grandparents' home when you visit.

- If temporary medicines seem to be piling up on a countertop for family members during flu season, gate the doorway to the room or lock the door. Concentrate on having all medicines in that one room to keep things under control.

- Consider a door alarm for those times when your guard is down.

☐ See Appendix 2 for a list of highly toxic household products and most common toxins. Two common but not so obvious toxins are antifreeze and oil of wintergreen. Read through the list. —It might surprise you.

☐ During your child's early years, try to live with a minimal number of toxic products in your home. One detergent, one dishwashing liquid, one all-purpose spray, and a scouring powder—these four seem easily manageable. Just throw out the extra stuff and start fresh later.

☐ Airborne toxins are also a danger to be aware of in your home.

- Make sure your home is well ventilated while painting or using other toxic chemicals.
- Keep the family away from home for several hours after having it treated for insect or pest control.
- If you suspect asbestos or radon gas in your home do not hesitate to have the appropriate tests conducted and any follow-up modifications made.
- Regularly clean filters in heaters and air conditioners. Mold and dust are often the cause for a chronic "runny nose."

Chapter Four

Childproofing Room by Room

After familiarizing you with the more common child-proofing concerns, it's time to move on to more specific room hazards.

The following is a room-by-room checklist designed with your and your child's best interests in mind. Each room presents detailed safety guidelines for you to follow in a number of areas, among them equipment, furniture, appliances, and living habits. Do not try to do it all at once. Take your time and go through the rooms slowly. Use the checklist as a guide, but do not disregard any unique qualities of your house which may not have been covered in this chapter. Trust your instincts. Know your house. Do not assume that anything you feel might pose a danger would not. Assume that it might and childproof accordingly.

Again, we urge you to take advantage of the device-count list at the back of this book to help you keep track of the devices you may wish to purchase.

KITCHEN

You guessed it! The most dangerous room in the house awaits your careful inspection. The kitchen is the first and most time-consuming room on your home tour. Take notes, tally your hardware needs, and make time to complete the job. Check every cubbyhole for hidden dangers such as sharp scissors, corkscrews, or insect bait. You may be surprised, even overwhelmed. If the job appears too big, do what you can and gate the doorway. Simply make it a strict rule to never allow small children in the kitchen.

DRAWERS

☐ Try to centralize dangerous utensils and other hazardous items in one or two drawers. Latch these drawers and teach your child "danger" when curiosity prompts him to try them.

☐ Place all knives in the childproof drawers. Butcher blocks and magnetic knife holders still pose a threat to "climbers." A few other dangers to include in latched drawers are foil and plastic wraps in boxes with serrated edges, toothpicks, and matches.

☐ Pull all drawers out. Make sure they have a safety catch preventing them from falling to the floor.

☐ Slide a yardstick down a row of drawer handles to keep a toddler from opening drawers.

CABINETS

☐ Move breakable glass items up high and plastics, pots, and pans down low.

☐ Food and heavy items should be kept out of reach. Appliances, especially those with sharp parts, need to be off-limits as well.

☐ After rearranging, consider latches for the reachable cabinets that contain hazards. Carefully examine the structure of your cabinets before shopping for latches. Not all latches work in every cabinet.

☐ Consider the possibility of providing your child with a cupboard of his own. Keep plastic cups, lightweight kitchen items, and kitchen toys inside for the curious explorer.

☐ If you store things under the sink, make sure they are nontoxic, nonfood items. Try placing a garbage container under the sink, keeping the cabinet latched at all times.

RANGE AND OVEN

☐ Preheat the oven. Then check the oven door to assure adequate door insulation.

☐ If stove knobs are within reach, try removing the knobs or purchasing a commercial shield to discourage the reaching child.

☐ Turn pot handles to the rear of the stove and cook on back burners.

☐ Do not store any food or snacks above the stove.

☐ Teach the meaning of "hot" at an early age. Use red dot stickers as a teaching tool, associating red with "danger" and "hot."

☐ Have a pot lid, box of baking soda, or salt handy to snuff out a small pan fire.

MICROWAVE OVEN

☐ Keep microwave doors clean, especially around the seal.

☐ Turn the appliance off before opening.

☐ Have a damaged seal replaced promptly.

DISHWASHER

☐ Start the dishwasher promptly after filling the soap cup. Beware of small children investigating the detergent and sneaking a taste.

SMALL APPLIANCES

☐ Make sure all electrical appliances are in good repair.

☐ Check cords and make sure they are tucked up and in back of each machine.

☐ Unplug appliances after each use and never operate one near a sink.

☐ Keep your kitchen simple. The more appliances you collect, the more risk you add to your lifestyle.

REFRIGERATOR

☐ Never move or store a refrigerator without removing the door. An abandoned or unused refrigerator can be a tempting—and fatal—hiding place for small children.

☐ Check to make sure you do not have any toxins in the refrigerator. Batteries, vitamins, and alcohol are frequent hidden poisons lurking in the refrigerator.

☐ Latch the refrigerator door if your child frequently opens it.

☐ Do not leave open cans in the refrigerator. Some canners still use lead soldering materials which can leach into foods and juices that are opened and stored improperly.

GARBAGE DISPOSAL

☐ These useful tools pose an electrical hazard since they are located near water. If you have one, latch the cabinet under the sink. Be sure there is a ground fault device used in the connection.

☐ *No trash compactors* until all your children are five and over. Small children can fit into trash compactors. Four-year-olds are capable of finding the key and starting the machine. Do not take the risk. If you have one, do not use it. Store the key in your jewelry box or other safe place.

MISCELLANEOUS

☐ Keep stools and other "steps" out of the kitchen.

☐ When cleaning up the inevitable broken glass:

- Sweep all visible glass into a pile.
- Use a wet paper towel to gather the finest shards remaining.
- Discard glass wrapped up in a newspaper or tucked into a milk carton to avoid further hazard.

☐ Use insect sprays and traps carefully. Traps should be well hidden and sprays used cautiously, preferably when children are out of the house.

☐ Plan to install reliable smoke alarms.

☐ Clean up spills promptly so that your toddler won't slip on a slick area.

BEDROOMS

☐ Add smoke alarms to all your bedrooms. They are inexpensive and easy to maintain.

☐ Store jewelry out of reach. Costume jewelry, beads, pins, and rings all have a history of injury.

☐ Commit yourself to the rule of never leaving your baby unattended on a standard-height bed. Throw a blanket on the floor for a safe nap away from home if there are no dogs or other pets loose in the house.

☐ Use knob covers to childproof any doorways leading to bathrooms.

☐ If you smoke in the bedroom, refrain when the children are around. Never smoke in bed.

☐ Consider placing a doorknob cover on your guest-room door and instructing visitors to keep the door closed during their stay.

☐ Fireplaces need adequate hearth, screen, and closure.

☐ No accessible ashtrays or loose matches.

☐ Hang belts, neckties, and similar accessories with the safety of your child in mind.

DINING ROOM

Liquor cabinets, good china, sharp cutlery, and swinging chandeliers are the main hazards to deal with in the dining room.

☐ Rearrange your wine rack, liquor cabinet, or bar. Moving liquor from low to high may be all that you need to reduce the risk.

☐ Commercial devices may be a worthwhile investment to keep a cabinet latched or a bar gated off.

☐ Consider keeping a "dry" home for a few years.

☐ Move the good china or use a latch to secure the cabinet doors. It is possible on some pieces of furniture to remove the handles. If these options do not work, try tying a large belt around the entire cabinet to secure the doors in a closed position.

☐ Raise low-hanging chandeliers.

☐ Avoid using tablecloths during your child's first few years. Just one pull can topple the candlesticks and ruin the evening.

☐ Common toxins in the dining room include: scented candles, colorful-tipped matches, liquor, and old pewter dishes or "craft show" pottery that may leach lead.

LIVING ROOM/FAMILY ROOM

☐ Fireplaces need adequate hearth, screen, and closure.

☐ Partitions and decorative screens should be removed for a few years. Mark mirrored or glass dividers with artwork or stickers at your child's eye level.

☐ If you have a piano, remember to close the lid and tuck in the bench.

☐ Do not use reclining chairs during your child's early years (birth to age three). Watch this especially while visiting. Most accidents occur while a child is left unattended.

☐ Move all breakable items such as trinkets, vases, dried-flower arrangements, lighters, and ashtrays to higher ground.

☐ Test all bookcases and shelving units for potential tipping hazard. Give each piece of furniture a shake. Remove hazardous shelves or fasten unit to the wall using "L" braces or a couple of secure screws.

☐ Pack away or remove any valuable books within your child's reach. A toddler can easily de-shelve even the most tightly packed bookshelf. Try filling the bottom shelf with your child's books and toys for a short period until this phase passes. By eighteen months a child can learn and understand proper book care. Set rules and teach children to respect books at an early age.

☐ Arrange your furniture with your child in mind. Use caution when positioning rocking chairs, hanging furniture, and any piece containing glass.

ELECTRONIC EQUIPMENT

Every home differs in the kinds of furniture and decorations found in these two rooms. However, many people locate televisions, videocassette recorders, stereo systems, and personal computers in this area of the home. These valuables usually present a dilemma for new parents.

Consider moving all such equipment out of your child's reach. If you choose to locate the television on a wall unit, make sure the cabinet or shelf is well ventilated, and that the wall unit is sturdy and able to hold this equipment safely in place.

A Velcro device may aid in securing a stereo lid in place.

A plastic typewriter cover or a homemade drape will keep little hands from stashing small objects in the cassette openings or disk drive openings on your computer. This developmental stage will pass quickly if rules are set early and consistently enforced.

FIREARMS

Household displays of handguns are not wise! Tragic firearm accidents occur at home more frequently than we would like to believe. Handguns kept handy to ward off intruders more often end up accidentally killing innocent victims. The National Safety Council reported that in 1987 forty children under age five were killed by a firearm in the home. The following checklist suggests safety measures for families that own firearms:

☐ Store guns up high, unloaded, with the safety lock engaged, and separate from ammunition.

☐ Beware of guns that are advertised as safe, including air guns, target pistols, BB guns, and flare guns. A projectile from these guns could kill a small child at close range.

☐ Always handle a gun as if it were loaded.

☐ Do not demonstrate guns in front of small children, yet avoid instilling fear. At an appropriate age, the proper function of a gun needs to be explained.

☐ Avoid allowing play guns that look like the real thing. Imitation revolvers and laser tag guns fall into this category.

☐ When visiting grandparents, childcare providers, or playtime friends, do not hesitate to inquire about any handguns stored in their home.

BATHROOMS

Common sense will confirm the list of hazards found in any bathroom. Inconvenience and frustration may overwhelm you at this point in your home tour. Hang in there. Keep reminding yourself that children grow up.

Most of the risk found in the bathroom can be eliminated early with safety lessons and a few strict rules. For now, read through the following checklist and make the necessary changes. The entire family will benefit from your efforts.

☐ Consider a doorknob cover on the outside of bathroom doors. This will act as a deterrent for the exploring child, allowing you time to catch up and provide a distraction.

☐ If you use throw rugs, make sure they have rubberized bottoms.

☐ Hang washables inside the tub or shower so water does not drip on the floor.

☐ Purchase bathroom supplies in unbreakable containers.

☐ Use paper cups and change toothbrushes after illness to keep the "bug" from going around.

☐ If you use disposable razors, locate them out of reach and dispose of them carefully. Gather any other sharp objects like scissors or tweezers and store them properly as well.

☐ Hang unbreakable mirrors and a towel rack at your child's level. If you keep necessary supplies down low, they will not have to climb. Caution: No clothes hooks at eye level. Keep them at arm's reach.

☐ Electric razors, blow dryers, electric curlers or toothbrushes become a hazard in the bathroom when used near a water source like a sink, toilet, or tub. Make sure your electrical outlets and appliances are safe. Disengage plugs after each use. Make a rule that no one touches these appliances with wet hands.

☐ This is a room where you will probably need a box to gather toxins. Medicines, caustic cleaning products, and cosmetics need to be organized and childproofed.

☐ Unfortunately, some insects thrive in this moist environment. If you find it necessary to use insect traps or sprays, make an effort to hide traps and use sprays as sparingly as possible.

TOILETS

☐ Keep lid down.

☐ Consider a lid latch for toilets, especially in bathrooms that are not frequently used.

☐ Avoid colored toilet bowl cleaners.

☐ Have a child's step stool available with skidproof rubber treads.

BATHTUBS

☐ Purchase a spout cover to pad any accidental falls.

☐ Check bathwater (80 degrees is comfortable). Test the water with your elbow.

☐ Avoid tub-sitting devices. They tend to provide a false sense of security. Some parents drop their guard while a child is sitting in one of the safety devices.

☐ Unplug the phone at bathtime or turn on the phone answering machine.

☐ Avoid harsh bubble baths.

☐ Place anti-slip stickers or a rubber mat on the bottom of any tub or shower that does not already have a slip-proof surface. (Installation tip: clean the tub thoroughly before sticking adhesive. Use rubbing alcohol to assure a clean, dry surface.)

☐ Encourage small children to replace soap in the soap dish and clear out soap scum buildup.

☐ If you are redecorating or have the opportunity to choose your fixtures, look for L-shaped handlebars to support a safe exit. Purchase nonslip fixtures and safety glass to minimize risks.

NURSERY

☐ If your nursery is not within hearing range of every room in your house, an intercom would be a worthwhile investment.

☐ Choose a safe, high location for placement of a vaporizer.

☐ Make sure the cord to the vaporizer is not within a child's reach and is not a tripping hazard. Also, periodically check the condition of the cord.

☐ Clean your vaporizer frequently.

☐ Avoid a used vaporizer. When shopping, choose a cool-mist appliance.

☐ Add an extra smoke alarm to this special room.

☐ Keep your baby's changing materials out of reach, especially baby powders and cornstarch (they could cause a respiratory arrest if a significant amount of powder is inhaled into an infant's lungs). Harmless-looking wipes and towelettes do not claim to be nontoxic and often contain alcohol, ether, and other undesirable ingredients.

☐ "Tot Finder" fire identification stickers are not recommended for windows. Fire rescuers enter burning buildings on their hands and knees. A sticker placed on the outside, lower portion of your nursery door will be more likely to be seen in such an emergency.

☐ If you use a decorative night light, make sure it is out of reach.

☐ Use sandpaper on the bottom of new leather-soled shoes to prevent slipping. Avoid "jingle bell" shoelace devices. They are a choking hazard as well as bothersome for most parents.

☐ Some ingenious children open drawers and use them as steps to climb the bureau. Suggestions:

- Latch bottom drawers.
- Secure lightweight dressers to the wall with hook and eyes or a couple of nails. L-shaped braces are also available in hardware stores for the same purpose.
- Another option is to buy a more secure piece of furniture.

☐ Clear all clutter off the floor at night, just in case you are called to comfort a babe in distress.

☐ Parents of little boys: Avoid using squirt-protector devices on child-size toilet seats. Injuries have been associated with this hard plastic attachment. If a child is old enough to be toilet trained, he is old enough to point himself down. This device is not necessary.

ROOMS TO BE KEPT OFF-LIMITS

We strongly recommend that parents set firm rules and keep the following rooms inaccessible to small children: dens, sewing rooms, workshops and hobby centers, attics, garages, laundry rooms, home gyms, and unfinished basements. This is where a doorknob cover, locking device, or alarm could come in handy.

☐ Install locks on all doors leading outside.

☐ If you must allow small children in these rooms, consider having a playpen filled with special toys, or a special table and chair. Take time to point out "danger" and teach safety lessons when the opportunity arises.

☐ Consider locked cabinets or drawers and remind yourself to keep things stored safely.

☐ Consider building a chicken-wire cage, secured with a lock, around all yard tools, toxins, and hazardous materials in your garage.

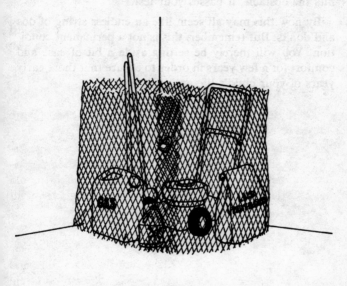

Added Prevention in the Garage

Chicken wire and a padlock around hazardous items can provide an added measure of safety in your garage.

☐ Check ventilation in workshop areas and garage. Avoid idling your car in the garage, especially when the family is strapped in place.

☐ Garage door openers are a well-known cause of accidents. Be sure the remote switch is kept out of reach. (Try locking it in the glove compartment.) Occasionally check the reverse function on the door to make sure it is working properly. You can do this by propping a trash can under the closing door. If the door reverses when it hits the obstacle, it passes your test.

By now this may all seem like an endless string of dos and don'ts. But remember, this is not a permanent condition. You will merely be setting aside a bit of ease and comfort for a few years in order to ensure that those early years of your child's life are safe ones.

Chapter Five

Nursery Equipment Safety Check

You may have been wondering why the nursery portion of the room-by-room checklist was so short. Products associated with the nursery are critical to your child's safety and warrant a chapter all their own.

New parents have many decisions to make when planning for their baby's arrival. In the past, alerting oneself to the variety of products available and the safety measures associated with each has not been an easy task. This chapter outlines a complete safety checklist for all of your product and equipment needs during your child's first five years. It includes the dos and don'ts associated with cribs, bassinets and cradles, playpens, changing tables, diaper pails, toy chests, strollers, and more. Do not hesitate to take this checklist with you when shopping for new or used nursery equipment.

CRIBS AND ACCESSORIES

☐ Make sure the crib slats are spaced no more than 2⅜ inches (6 cm) apart to prevent your infant from slipping, feet first, through the slats.

Safe crib?

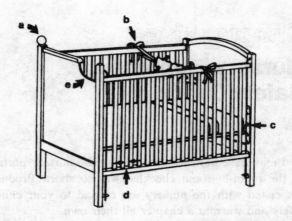

a. *Decorations like this post can easily catch on a child's cloth-ing and cause a choking hazard.*
b. *Crib gyms can pose a choking hazard.*
c. *Make sure the height of the mattress decreases as your child's height increases.*
d. *Slats should be no more than 2³⁄₈ inches apart.*
e. *Cut-out designs can pose the risk of entrapment.*

☐ The crib slats should be secure. Avoid any used cribs with missing slats or noticeable damage.

☐ Mattresses should fit securely. The mattress is too small if you can fit more than two fingers anywhere around its edge.

☐ Once assembled, give the crib a shake to make sure it is secure. Check mattress support hangers to see if they are correctly in place.

☐ Avoid cribs with corner posts that extend higher than ⁵⁄₈ inch. This design can act as a fatal hook catching a necklace or piece of clothing tied around a baby's neck. Saw the corner posts off if you need to make do with an older-model crib.

☐ Remove all plastic coverings surrounding a new crib mattress. Make sure never to use thin plastic trash or dry cleaning bags to line the mattress. Dispose of these plastics by tying them in knots and shoving them to the bottom of your trash can.

☐ Stay clear of cribs that have cut-out designs on either end. These areas pose the threat of head or hand entrapment.

☐ Remove any pillows or stuffed toys from your infant's crib. Continue to keep these items out of your toddler's crib. An older baby might try to use these objects as steps to climb over the side.

☐ Baby gyms strung across the crib should be removed once your child can push up on her hands and knees. Still better, avoid these kinds of toys altogether.

☐ Remove hanging crib toys and mobiles once your child can stand. They are not worth the risk of having her break and pull these objects into the crib.

☐ Crib hammocks are an accessory used to hold infants during their first three months. Follow manufacturer's guidelines for safe use and check recall notices if you plan to use this product.

☐ Rule of thumb for all infant and crib toys: Make sure there are no strings longer than 12 inches.

☐ Make sure the drop-side crib latches hold up securely in the raised position. Toddlers are notorious for reaching down and releasing the crib sides. If possible, avoid the simple foot releases that invite reaching hands or siblings to lower the crib side.

☐ When your child learns to stand, drop the mattress to its lowest level and remove the foam bumper pad. These pads become steps that children use to crawl up and out of the crib.

☐ If you do use bumper pads, make sure they fit all the way around the crib and attach in at least six different spots. Trim ties if they hang longer than 12 inches.

☐ The crib should be located with safety in mind. Avoid placing it near any lamps, dangling cords, windows, fans, heaters, or climbable furniture.

☐ Secondhand cribs are safe if they can be modified to meet the above requirements. Remember to check the label on paint cans if you decide to refinish the crib. Avoid old paint produced prior to 1978 and use a high-quality enamel.

☐ Before shopping for a used crib, crib devices, or crib toys, check recall notices.

☐ Check teething rails for brittle, splintered, rough or broken edges.

☐ Avoid crib decals that may peel off. Your baby could surprise you by peeling and taste-testing these decorations.

☐ If you have a crib-rocking toddler, be sure to check the sturdiness of your crib frequently and tighten all loose fittings.

☐ When your baby begins climbing, you can take added safety measures by having some soft pillows and stuffed animals in the "fall zone" surrounding the crib just in case.

☐ Crib extenders can be purchased and placed on crib sides, adding height to prevent falls.

BASSINETS AND CRADLES

☐ Shop for wide-based models. Make sure your bassinet or cradle seems stable, with a firm bottom and well put together.

☐ Make sure mattress pads have a snug fit and use the two-finger mattress check described earlier. Excess fluff may appear cozy, but it is not a good idea when planning for your newborn.

☐ Look for any rough edges, protruding staples, or other hazards that could injure your child.

☐ Keeping in mind that all babies have their own developmental timetable, use common sense and manufacturer's guidelines to tell you when it is time to put away the cradle. (Rough estimate: three months.)

☐ If the bassinet you choose has folding legs, make sure that safety locks are provided to guard against accidental collapse while in use.

☐ Remember when using secondhand products to check for loose screws, bolts, and old, chipped paint.

☐ Keep the crib safety guidelines in mind.

YOUTH BEDS AND BED GUARDS

When your baby shows signs of trying to climb out of the crib it is time for a bed. This age varies for each child but a general rule for eliminating the crib is when the height of the side of the crib is less than 3/4 of your child's height.

Parents may choose to throw a mattress on the floor, purchase a specially designed youth bed, or modify a standard bed with side guards. The bed guards have extension legs that fit between the mattress and the box springs. These devices create a barrier along the side of the bed to keep your child from rolling onto the floor. Regardless of your choice, be prepared for your child to wander during the changeover. Night lights and uncluttered floors will help make this a safe transition period.

☐ Never use an electric blanket on your toddler's bed if there is still a chance of bedwetting.

☐ Bed guards vary in length. When shopping for a bed guard, purchase the longer models.

☐ Keep in mind the crib safety checklist and continue to trust your common sense when using secondhand youth beds and bed guards.

☐ Bunk beds may seem appealing but are not a good choice for a safe first bed.

PLAYPENS AND AREA ENCLOSURES

☐ Do not use old wooden accordion-style expandable enclosures with diamond-shaped openings. These area enclosures have been recalled because they pose the risk of head entrapment.

☐ There are many new area enclosures; some are open, corral-like structures, and others resemble small tents. The enclosures appear safe as long as you remember never to leave your child unattended. There will come a day when your toddler will stack the blocks and climb out or lift the side and crawl under.

☐ If you choose to use a drop-side playpen, follow the manufacturer's advice and remember never to leave a side down in the lowered position. When a side is left down, a gap is formed between the side and the floor panel. Infants have been known to roll into this mesh gap and suffocate. Older toddlers have also climbed into the playpen and pinched fingers on the unlocked hinge mechanism.

☐ When shopping for a new playpen, look for products bearing the voluntary safety standard seal of the Juvenile Products Manufacturers Associates (JPMA).

☐ Look for mesh netting that has a tight weave (less than ¼ inch openings). Small buttons on a baby's clothing could catch in the weave.

☐ Check used playpens for torn vinyl, exposed metal, or rough edges. Teething children have been known to chew off torn pieces, which then pose a choking hazard.

☐ Slats on playpens should be no more than 2⅜ inches in width. Check for snug pad fit as described for crib mattress.

☐ When your baby can pull to a stand, remove large toys, bumper pads, infant seats, or large blocks from inside the playpen. They can be used for climbing out.

☐ Avoid tying any crib gyms across the top or along the side of the playpen. The concerned parent should realize that tied-up toys are not a wise choice. Remember the twelve-inch rule for any cords or ties.

☐ If staples are used to attach the mesh material to the floorboard, make sure none are loose or missing.

☐ Keep tabs on loose threads or tears. Trim threads and repair holes before allowing your child back in the playpen or enclosure.

NURSERY CHANGING TABLES

☐ Changing tables are not a necessity. If you choose to use one, make sure it has accessible shelves, a reliable safety strap, and 6- to 8-inch side ridges.

☐ Look for a changing table with a wide base. Make sure it is something an older child cannot climb up or tip over on herself.

☐ Avoid storing your child's medicines on the changing table shelves.

☐ Check the stability of your changing table periodically as your child grows.

☐ Remember never to leave your baby on the changing table without a strap and at least one hand.

☐ Keep baby-changing materials out of reach, especially baby powders, cornstarch, creams, and safety pins.

☐ Move furniture away from the changing table and make sure that older babies cannot push off from the wall or any other objects.

DIAPER PAILS

☐ Keep your diaper pail tightly sealed and out of reach. The cake deodorizers, plastic bag liners, and liquid used to soak cloth diapers all pose a threat to curious children.

☐ Try moving the pail into a childproofed closet or to the top of a high bureau.

☐ Instead of using thin plastic trash can liners, try to replace them with the crinkly plastic or paper shopping bags found in some grocery and department stores.

☐ If you must use a cake deodorizer, shop for the brands that are encased in plastic.

TOY CHESTS

☐ There are three potential accidents related to toy boxes and toy chests:

- The lid may fall when babies use the chest to pull themselves up.
- A child may suffocate if trapped inside without ventilation.
- Injuries may result from falling against corners and edges. To avoid these kinds of problems, check for JPMA certification safety seals when shopping for a new toy chest.

☐ Make sure that any toy box you choose has ventilation holes that cannot be blocked if it is placed against the wall. At the same time, make sure that it has ventilation when the lid is closed. If necessary, drill some small holes as a precaution.

☐ Remove the lid or install spring-loaded lid supports on any toy chests, footlockers, or trunks with free falling lids. Open chests, bins, or sliding-door toy boxes are safe alternatives.

☐ If your toy chest has a hinged lid, make sure it uses a support that is tight and will keep the lid in place at any level.

☐ Check for sharp corners, rough edges, and loose screws or splinters.

☐ Pad blunt corners and avoid locating the box near staircases or heavily traveled areas in your home.

☐ Avoid placing toy chests on smooth, slippery surfaces, waxed floors, or throw rugs.

☐ Remove from your home any old toy chests or trunks that have a latch on them.

PACIFIERS

☐ Make sure your baby's pacifier has no ribbon, string, cord, or yarn attached.

☐ Never tie a pacifier around your baby's neck or pin it to her clothing.

☐ Make sure that the shield around the nipple of your pacifier is large and firm enough so it cannot fit into your baby's mouth.

☐ The shield should have ventilation holes so that a child can breathe if does get into her mouth.

☐ Check the condition of the pacifier frequently. Make sure it has no torn parts that may break off and pose a choking hazard.

☐ Boil pacifiers frequently to avoid episodes of infection ranging from common cold to thrush.

CHILDREN'S CLOTHING

☐ Remove any thin dry cleaner's plastic covering from your children's clothes.

☐ Remove unnecessary long strings from clothing and caps.

☐ Be sure clothes are not tight or binding, especially around neck, arms, and legs.

☐ ·Check buttons regularly. They should be sewn on tightly.

☐ Check for loose threads that can get wrapped around little fingers or toes.

☐ Shop for flame-resistant sleepwear with no added chemicals—particularly TRIS, a chemical banned in the late 1970s. Follow manufacturer's instructions on laundry care to retain resistancy. It is easy to forget to follow the instructions.

☐ To reduce the chances of car-related accidents as your children grow, remember the value of light-colored clothing and reflector tape.

☐ Beware of perfumed diapers, clothes, soaps, and fabric softeners which may cause an allergic reaction. If a rash develops, discontinue using such products.

INFANT SEATS AND CARRIERS

☐ The seat should have a wide, sturdy base.

☐ If the seat does not have rubber, nonskid tabs, attach some rough-surfaced bathtub adhesive strips to the underside.

☐ Always use the safety belts (including the crotch strap) and make sure these straps work with ease.

☐ Avoid setting these seats on tables, drainboards, beds, or chairs. If you must arrange the seat up high, stay within arm's reach of the baby and keep in mind that as soon as the baby becomes more physically active, the seat should be left on the ground.

☐ Make sure all supporting devices lock securely. One model has wire bars that snap into plastic notches in the back.

☐ For added comfort, use safety head cushions that surround the baby's head with padding or rolled towels tucked on either side for support.

☐ Never use these products as substitute car seats. One exception is the approved infant car seat that is designed to be a carrier as well.

SWINGS AND HOPPERS

Swings and hoppers vary in safe design. Use common sense when shopping for these items and check recall notices before buying used models.

☐ The hoppers that clamp tightly above a doorway molding are the most secure models when used according to manufacturer's directions.

☐ Do not put your baby in a hopper or swing before she is strong enough. Check recommended age and weight guidelines for correct use.

☐ Absolutely never move out of sight of your child while she is in a hopper or swing.

☐ Swings that come equipped with small toys need to be checked regularly for any loose or small parts.

☐ Always fasten all safety harnesses, including the crotch strap.

WALKERS

☐ When using a walker, make sure your child is kept away from stairways, kitchens, and fireplaces.

☐ To avoid falls, never allow your baby to wander near stairs or other hazards that pose falling potential.

☐ To keep your baby out of off-limits rooms:

- gate the doorway
- close the door
- lay down a 2 × 4-inch board across the doorway so that your baby cannot push the walker into the other room.

☐ Make sure your walker has a wide wheel base and secure seating to prevent tipping.

☐ Avoid X-frame walkers. If you already have this design, make sure it has protective plastic sleeves over the coil springs and guards over any parts that could pinch.

☐ Never allow the baby and walker to move out of your sight, especially outdoors.

☐ Keep floors clear of obstacles, including toys and loose carpets.

☐ Check walker for rough edges, torn padding, or a worn-out seat.

☐ Follow manufacturer's directions for safe usage, including appropriate age and weight limits.

☐ Never pick up and carry a walker with your child in it.

☐ Walkers should not be used in rooms with a space heater.

HIGH CHAIRS AND HOOK-ON SEATS

☐ Falls can be prevented by using all of the chair's safety straps and closely supervising your child during high chair use. Do not depend on the tray as a restraining device.

☐ It is not wise to use a high chair if your baby cannot sit up comfortably.

☐ Collapsed high chairs or tip-overs can occur when older

babies rock the chair or push off from a wall or other stable surface. Never leave your child unattended in a high chair.

☐ When shopping for a high chair look for:

- the JPMA safety-approved certification seal
- sturdy legs (avoid wheels)
- design that allows easy in-and-out use
- sturdy straps for both waist and crotch which are independent of the tray.
- rigid locking devices on collapsible models.
- no sharp edges, exposed holes, or torn vinyl.
- a tray finish that will not peel or bubble.

☐ Know where your child's hands are before you attach or detach the tray.

☐ Carry with you a strap of harness to use on public high chairs, grocery carts, and strollers that lack adequate restraining straps.

☐ Never allow your child to stand in or climb into the high chair unattended.

☐ Teach older brothers and sisters not to climb on the high chair when the baby is in it.

☐ Discourage bacteria and strap deterioration by keeping the high chair clean.

☐ Avoid older high chairs with plastic caps that can be pulled off, posing a choking hazard. If you already have such a model, tape caps in place.

☐ Childproof slippery seats by adding a few adhesive tub strips or stickers.

☐ Avoid hook-on high chairs altogether. If you must use them, make sure you find a model with table clamps. The push-off potential is too risky, especially when placed near another chair. Follow manufacturer's guidelines for safe use and remember never to use these chairs on glass-topped or shaky tables.

STROLLERS AND BUGGIES

☐ Avoid unfolding and collapsing your stroller or buggy near your baby. There are too many parts that could pinch.

☐ When making a stop, use both brakes and never leave your child unattended.

☐ Always use waist and crotch strap. Replacement straps are available from the manufacturer or your local hardware store. Look for straps that fasten with ease.

☐ Prevent tipping by checking reclining positions and purchasing a stable stroller with a wide base. Avoid hanging bags on handles. Be extra careful when pushing uphill and do not allow younger children to push the stroller without your guiding hand.

☐ Make sure your new stroller has the JPMA safety-approved certification seal.

☐ Check recall notices before purchasing a new stroller or buggy.

☐ Avoid sharp edges or protrusions.

☐ Since buggies and strollers are pushed in front of you, be careful when pushing your child into traffic or crowded areas.

FRONT CARRIERS AND BACKPACKS

☐ Front carriers are generally used for infants and should provide adequate head and shoulder support. Provide neck support with a spare hand if you choose to use a front carrier during your child's early months.

☐ Select front carriers and backpacks with comfortable shoulder straps and leg openings large enough to avoid chafing or cutting off the circulation.

☐ Be sure to follow manufacturer's guidelines for safe use and appropriate age and weight restrictions. Never use backpacks until your baby is strong enough, which should be at approximately five months. Check manufacturer's instructions.

☐ Check recall notices before purchasing a used carrier.

☐ If you are using a secondhand carrier, check to make sure it is in good repair. Discard torn, frayed, mildewed, or out-of-shape packs. Occasionally check your carrier for ripped seams, torn straps, or any other signs of deterioration. Repair or discard worn carriers.

☐ Do not leave your child unattended in a backpack with a stand.

☐ Always use a restraining strap.

☐ If you need to lean over or stoop down while wearing a carrier, always remember to bend from the knees to protect your child from a serious fall.

☐ Keep your baby's fingers free of joints and parts that could pinch.

☐ Make sure your pack frame is adequately padded and provides a comfortable resting place for your baby's head while sleeping.

□ Look for sturdy construction. Leg openings should not be big enough for your baby to slip through.

□ As your baby grows and becomes restless inside the backpack, try holding a leg for added security.

□ When purchasing a carrier, look for:

- Enough depth to support your baby's neck.
- Appropriate-size leg openings.
- Sturdy materials and good workmanship.
- Padded coverings over the metal frame.

INFANT FORMULA AND BABY FOOD

□ Do not store powdered formula or boxed cereal in the refrigerator.

□ Try to purchase products with the latest expiration date.

□ Store products in a cool area. Avoid extreme heat or cold so that essential nutrients are not harmed.

□ Always read packages carefully. Never dilute ready-to-feed formulas. When reconstituting a product, carefully add the proper amounts of water to assure adequate nutritional content.

□ Rinse the top of any can of infant formula and use a sterile can opener to open the can.

□ Always check the vacuum seal on baby food jar lids. If the top appears to be "popped up," don't buy that jar.

□ Never put leftover baby food back into the jar. Also, do not feed out of a jar. If you do, discard the leftovers. The enzymes in a baby's saliva will break down the nutrients.

□ Babies under the age of one should never be fed honey. Honey contains bacterial spores that could cause botulism in the intestinal tracts of infants.

TOOTHBRUSHES AND TOOTHPASTE

☐ Choose a brush with a small head to avoid mouth injury.

☐ Place a small amount of toothpaste on the brush and teach your child to rinse thoroughly.

☐ Use of fluoride toothpaste should be monitored carefully, especially in areas that have fluoridated water. Small children have a tendency to swallow toothpaste and this could have a toxic effect on their systems.

BOTTLE WARMERS AND FEEDING DISHES

☐ Serving food and formula at room temperature is the easiest choice. Household warmers are generally a safe choice. Check for automatic thermostats, insulated sides, and UL (Underwriters Listing.)

☐ Water-heated dishes are a safer choice than electrically heated dishes. (There is no risk of tripping on a cord.) Experts, however, indicate that heating baby food is not necessary.

☐ Never leave a metal feeding spoon in an electrically heated feeding dish while it is warming. The spoon can become too hot for a baby.

☐ Despite advertising, never warm a bottle in a microwave oven. Microwave heat is very uneven, and the temperature of the liquid could vary within the bottle. So while the bottle may feel cool when you test it, it is possible that there are spots hot enough to scald a baby's mouth.

Chapter Six
Babes in Toyland

Toy safety must take priority as one of our greatest concerns. The deception of consumers through slick marketing and questionable industry standards has led us to believe that no toy is safe unless it passes your inspection first. Buyer beware: Toyland is full of little tin soldiers with sharp rough edges, toy guns with dangerous flying projectiles and loud "Bangs," flammable dolls, parts that present a choking hazard, and electrical nightmares.

Taking responsibility for toy safety is a difficult task for many reasons. For one thing, toy safety guidelines are based upon the developmental age of the average child. Problems arise when our kids develop earlier or later than the norm. The most frequent problem occurs when toys that are safe for your five-year-old are at the same time a potential danger in the hands of a playful little sibling or neighbor. This dilemma is often frightening for parents who suddenly find themselves surrounded by unsafe toys when baby number two comes along. Yet toy industry manufacturers advertise "safe" toys using specific age guidelines on their products.

Sophisticated packaging, marketing, and promotion can fool the unwary parent. It is difficult not to be influenced by all of the subliminal messages that we are exposed to. Impulse buying frequently overrides common-sense shopping. Unfortunately, there are many popular toys that are available and advertised as safe, yet have caused death and injury. The toy industry is as concerned with profits as any other segment of business, and many unsafe products slip through the cracks.

Throughout the last twenty years, well-known toy manufacturing companies have been producing toys that have killed or injured a number of children. We ask ourselves why these toys are still available and found in many homes.

In 1982, a large toy manufacturer received a warning from the Consumer Product Safety Commission (CPSC) about the danger of their crib gyms, a soft, stuffed version strung with ribbon. Two years later, a ten-month-old infant strangled to death on one of these crib gyms. It was not until 1986, four years and two deaths later, that the 1.6 million crib toys were recalled. (Beware: this type of crib gym is still widely available.)

Many classic toys that we grew up with, and associate happy memories with, are not especially safe either. For example, jacks and marbles can easily be swallowed. Favorites like balloons (when deflated), colorful beads, and cap guns are responsible for numerous injuries. These are just a few of the dangerous toys that have stood the test of time. As parents you may find yourselves rationalizing: "I grew up with these toys and nothing happened to me," or "My child would never stick something up his nose, he's too smart." The fact remains that accidents happen and we must take responsibility for protecting our children by allowing only safe toys in our homes.

Naturally parents are not the only ones who buy toys for children. There is also the problem of gifts. What can we do about these toys? There are no guarantees that

Avoid small toys and toys with small parts or sharp points. Check toys carefully before making any purchases and remember to discard broken, irreparable toys.

they are safe, yet we can hardly take them away once the present is opened.

There is also the problem of those toys found in party favor bags, gum-ball machines, candy boxes, and fast-food meal boxes. These toys are frequently unsafe and catch us off guard. Again, as parents the responsibility is ours to provide a safe choice for our children.

Eventually all children grow up and begin asserting their independence. Once they learn to ride "the big toy," a bicycle, our responsibilities increase. We must consider major toy-related expenses including the purchase of safe bicycles, routine maintenance, and proper safety equipment such as helmets and reflective vests. We must also teach safe road rules and make sure they are followed.

Can we trust our government agencies to do enough? Many doubts come to mind when we consider that unsafe toys continue to be manufactured. For example, ingredients used to make toys are not always safe for children who chew them, nor are they nonflammable. If in fact more can be done to ensure safe toys for our children it is up to us to contact our legislators and take steps to foster change.

Toys are exciting, enjoyable learning tools for our children. We have the right to expect safe toys but the ultimate responsibility is ours. It is a difficult but manageable job. The following checklists are here to help you. Our best advice is to monitor toy play, be prepared, and trust your common sense.

TOY USE AND STORAGE

☐ Keep a file of all your toys. Save a portion of the packaging from each toy. Staple the price tag to it or record the price, date of purchase, and manufacturer's name somewhere on the packaging. Store all the wrappers in a large manila envelope or file folder. Commit yourself to reporting all toy-related accidents or potential accidents to the CPSC. This kind of record keeping will assure a complete and accurate report and possibly save lives.

☐ Check all toys regularly. Look for broken parts, sharp edges, loose pieces, and shoddy construction. Throw away broken and worn toys if they cannot be repaired.

☐ Organize your child's toys. If you find the task unmanageable, simply load some boxes with excess toys and store them. Periodically rotate the stored toys. You will find this method an easy way to check the condition of your toys on a regular basis. An added benefit will be your child's delightful look of surprise when the forgotten toys reappear.

☐ Have a special place for each toy. Shelves and baskets are best for most toys, with the toy box saved for larger toys, balls, and costumes. Your children will appreciate a sense of order, playing with toys that otherwise might sit buried at the bottom of a closet. An added benefit to this method is the ease with which you can hide harmful toys from younger children. Baskets filled with play jewelry, toy cars, action figures and dolls, snap-together blocks, crayons and other craft supplies can easily be stored up high when baby number two comes along. This will also provide you with the opportunity to throw in a safety lesson when your child asks, "But why, Mom?"

□ Organizing toys means keeping them picked up. Easier said than done. On bad days reserve a box or laundry basket for a run-through toy pickup. Sort things out later when the kids are in bed. Above all, keeping toys organized and picked up can prevent the number-one accident associated with toys: children falling off, over, or into toys.

TOY SAFETY GUIDELINES BY AGE LEVEL

BIRTH TO EIGHTEEN MONTHS

□ Avoid fluid-filled teethers. Incidents of a strong odor coming from a punctured teether and unexplained lethargy resulting from a similar leaking toy have been reported to the Consumer Product Safety Commission. Freeze a solid plastic model for the same soothing effect.

□ Avoid choking hazards that are not obvious! Babies have choked on objects such as rattles and pacifiers as large as 1 5/8 inches in diameter. This measurement may seem large, but an infant's mouth and throat are extremely flexible, able to stretch more than you might expect. Squeak toys with removable squeakers, teething beads, crib gyms, and plastic milk bottles filled with shapes all have a history of causing injury or death.

EIGHTEEN MONTHS TO THREE YEARS

☐ Avoid flammable toys, dolls with accessories, board games with small parts, toxic art projects, electrical toys, puzzles and snap-together blocks with small pieces, and costume jewelry.

☐ A rule of thumb for this age group is to stay clear of toys with any part small enough to be swallowed.

THREE TO FIVE YEARS

☐ Continue to avoid toys with small parts if your child still sucks a thumb or pacifier, or mouths toys. Keep in mind that toys advertised for three years and older may fall into this category.

☐ Pay close attention to age labeling on toy packages. Parents often try to challenge their children with advanced toys thinking they are better stimulated. Not so. The fact is that children develop at different rates. A three-year-old may be physically able to cope with an electric train, but his mental development may not be as advanced. Do not take chances when there are other appropriate toys to choose from—in this case, a wooden train set will do.

☐ Continue to refrain from purchasing any sharp or cutting toys, flammable dress-up clothes, shooting games, or electrical toys.

☐ Attach a safety flag on a flexible high rod to low-riding toys such as tricycles to increase their visibility.

☐ Rocking horses should be secured on a sturdy base and pass your inspection. Coil springs need to be covered with plastic sheaths to avoid pinching small fingers and toes.

TEACH YOUR CHILDREN ABOUT TOY SAFETY

Show your little ones how to recognize an unsafe toy and how to use their toys properly. Explain the importance of picking up their toys to prevent falls. As they grow, point out such hazards as:

- sharp or rough edges
- toys that poison, including rusty old toys with chipped paint
- toys and dress-up clothes that can catch fire
- toys (including long strings, loops, and small parts) that can choke a younger child
- dangerous toys that shoot things

It's a good idea to show older children how to report broken toys to an adult and get help if another child gets hurt.

As adults, we should set some specific rules regarding toys and play, bearing in mind that an older sibling's toys could pose special hazards and any play with these toys should be well supervised. Here are some standard rules to instill in your children as they grow:

- Always pick up toys and put them back in their place when you're through playing with them. (This is a tough one!)
- No throwing toys or sand.
- No toys in the mouth, nose, or ears.

- No giving "danger" toys to the baby or other small friends.
- No playing or riding in the street. Define the outdoor boundary.
- No diving from the stairs. (Superman costumes do have their drawbacks.)

WHAT PARENTS SHOULD KNOW BEFORE GOING TOY SHOPPING

SAFETY STANDARDS

Toy manufacturers in the United States follow certain guidelines in establishing what they advertise as a "safe" toy. These guidelines vary. Some are voluntary; others are mandated by law. To add to the confusion, legislation differs from state to state and country to country. Because manufacturers are not required to conduct premarketing testing, many unsafe toys slip through the cracks, resulting in a history of related injury. If this does not make you think twice about thoroughly checking all your children's toys, the following information may provide motivation:

☐ Parents should know that the manufacturer's compliance with the following safety standards is only voluntary:

- No strings longer than twelve inches.
- Squeeze toys and teethers should be large enough so that they cannot get lodged in a child's mouth.
- Toy-chest lids should stay open in any position.
- Crib gyms should be labeled to tell parents when to remove them. (Many other countries have banned them outright.)

Truncated Cylinder Test Tube

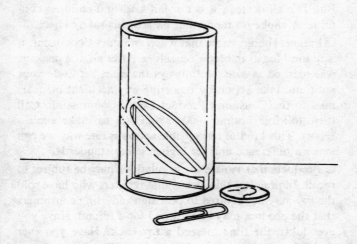

This device is used throughout the toy industry to determine which toys are too small for children three years and under. Developed by the Consumer Product Safety Commission based on recommendations by the American Academy of Pediatrics and the Toy Manufacturers of America, it is now being distributed on the retail level for home use.

☐ Parents must understand how age guidelines on toy packages are actually determined. The Toy Manufacturers of America created the "truncated cylinder test tube" (see illustration) to determine whether parts could cause choking. Any toy that has small parts able to fit into this tube is labeled "For ages three and up." The industry maintains these "voluntary safe standards" regardless of the fact that some three-to-five-year-olds can choke on these toys advertised as "safe." The testing device is a step in the right direction and is available to consumers.

But, like all devices, it is not fail-safe, and children continue to choke on items that passed this safety check.

☐ Parents should know that when an injury does occur, it is natural for us to blame ourselves. After all, the package was marked as safe. Not always the case! Set aside your guilt and take action by reporting any accident or near-miss to the Consumer Product Safety Commission. Call their toll-free hotline (800-638-CPSC) to make such a report. This kind of responsible action is one way we can make a difference and set higher safety standards.

☐ Products that violate toy regulations may be subject to recall. In practice, this means that retailers who have sold the toy may be required to post signs advising consumers that the product may be returned for a refund. Have you ever taken the time to send a toy back? Have you ever noticed recalls posted in your toy store?

☐ Many toys are marketed for a younger age group than the packaging may indicate. Evidence of this is seen in numerous advertising campaigns in which very young children are used to sell the product—certainly younger than the age indicated on the packaging. Several lawsuits have arisen over this issue, and the offending manufacturers have responded by adding a small disclaimer to the packaging which reads, "Regardless of age, this product is not intended for children who still put objects in their mouths." It is frustrating to know that respected toy manufacturers stoop to such deception to make the sale. Not many toy buyers would take the time to read the fine print on a toy package.

☐ Not all countries have safety requirements for their toys. On the other hand, Canada, Australia, and most European countries actually provide more stringent safety standards than does the United States.

☐ The label "nontoxic" does not guarantee that if the product bearing the label is eaten, a child will not experience a severe reaction. However, you can rest assured that your child will not be *fatally* poisoned by ingesting a nontoxic toy—hardly reassuring when your little cook eats the clay pie he created.

☐ Low-riding toys such as plastic tricycles cannot be seen by motorists and are associated with many fatal and serious accidents.

☐ Caution must be practiced when purchasing toys that might have flammable materials. Manufacturers are only regulated to meet 1954 flammable fabric requirements; though more stringent standards have been set up to provide flame retardancy for children's sleepwear, they are only voluntary.

☐ Ingredient labeling is not required on toys. Plastics (especially those containing polyvinyl chloride) emit toxic fumes when exposed to heat. Many plastics contain DEHP (di [2-ethylhexyl] phthalate), a carcinogen. Many plastic toys, pacifiers, and teething rings contain this cancer-causing ingredient. Nitrosamines also pose a cancer risk and may still be found in rubber nipples and pacifiers. Ferric ferrocyanide is another toxic ingredient to check for. It contains cyanide. Lead poisoning is still prevalent. Lead levels in paint are supposed to be limited to .06 percent. Since lead accumulates in a child's body, constant exposure to even low levels of lead can eventually cause a problem. If you are concerned about any of these ingredients and there is no mention of ingredients on the packaging, do not hesitate to contact the manufacturer and request the information.

TOY-BUYING TIPS

☐ Stay away from breakable, fragile toys during these years.

☐ Before purchasing a new toy, check it for durable construction. Do not hesitate to open a package and inspect a toy before you buy it.

☐ Consider the words "Use with adult supervision" to be a warning signal for a potentially unsafe toy.

☐ Avoid impulsive toy buying. If you really want the toy, promise yourself you will put it back on the shelf and walk around the store for a short time before you go back to buy it. Chances are you may never go back to get it.

☐ Avoid toys that never cite an appropriate age guideline. At the present time this is all toy manufacturers have given us to work with.

☐ Refrain from ordering mail-order toys that you cannot properly inspect before purchasing.

☐ Do not let the words "safe" or "complies with all applicable government safety regulations" keep you from making your own inspection. The same holds true for toys marked with special seals from Underwriters Laboratories (UL), The United States Testing Company, Inc. (USTC), or Good Housekeeping.

☐ For information on current toys that are appropriate for this age group you can contact the Consumer Product Safety Commission and request "Which Toys for Which Child: Selecting Suitable Toys Ages Birth Through Five."

☐ Avoid the following classic toys until your child is at least five:

- Teddy bears with glass or button eyes
- Small beads, including teething beads
- Splintered or old painted blocks
- Paints or felt pens that have no mention of toxicity
- Baby dolls with small plastic bottles and pacifiers, or with long hair
- Toy ovens, irons, or electric trains
- Battery-operated toys
- Metal-spring-covered jack-in-the-boxes
- Wooden toys that are not sanded smooth or have questionable paint content
- Spinning tops
- Collector dolls, especially those with china heads and small pins and tacks
- Toys filled with liquid substances
- Pop, dart, or cap guns
- Crib toys on a string

TIPS FOR ASSURING SAFE GIFTS

This kind of toy monitoring is not easy for the safety-minded parent. You will have to find the energy to plan ahead, organize, and commit yourself to the goal of assuring safe gifts. Tap your creative instincts along with the following suggestions:

☐ Do not hesitate to make a note on your party invitation such as "No toys, please." If people inquire, let them know of your concerns and ask for specific needs such as diapers, clothes, or a gift certificate.

☐ While your child is under two, you can easily screen out unsafe toys without much commotion. For the older child who receives an unsafe toy, you have several options:

- Monitor play.
- Explain why the toy is unsafe.
- Exchange the toy for a safe, agreeable alternative.
- If all else fails, put the new toy away for a few months and, if it is forgotten, get rid of it.

☐ Have theme parties suggesting a controllable inflow of gifts. For example, a "safety bear birthday party" or a book party in which everyone brings a book as a gift.

PARTY FAVORS AND PREMIUM TOYS

Many of these toys are responsible for serious childhood injuries. Please keep the following guidelines in mind.

☐ Avoid any toys that have small parts, sharp points, rough edges, propelled objects, or weak plastic construction. Monitor playtime and quickly weed these toys out of the toy collection.

☐ When purchasing fast-food meals for children, request the prize for three and under when the option is available.

☐ Report hazardous party favors and premium toys to the CPSC just as you would any other hazardous toy.

☐ Look for premium gifts that you can inspect before you make your purchase. Stickers, books, and decals are safe choices. Stay clear of the "surprise inside" packages.

BICYCLE SAFETY CHECKLIST

At some point during your child's development, you will discover that he and his bicycle are inseparable. Accidents involving children and bicycles occur with amazing frequency, especially during the warm-weather months. On the positive side, the majority of serious injuries can be avoided by the use of appropriate bicycle helmets.

☐ Choose bicycle helmets for you and your children that have a layer of hard Styrofoam-type material. Foam linings do not provide enough protection. The more expensive models tend to be the better choice. (See illustration.)

☐ Never bicycle without helmets. You cannot predict when another bicyclist or animal may tangle your spokes. Your good example is essential in creating safe habits for your children.

☐ Children under six months should not be taken on bicycles.

☐ No backpacks as carriers. Carry your precious cargo in a special child carrier mounted over the rear wheels of your bicycle.

☐ Limit bicycle child carriers to children up to forty pounds or four years old.

☐ When purchasing a bicycle child carrier:

- Make sure the seat has an adequate safety harness, a high back, a rear attachment to the adult bicycle for better balance, and a plastic safety shield to protect small feet.
- Purchase some safety accessories such as a fluorescent safety flag and a rearview mirror.
- Avoid yard-sale or thrift-shop specials. Parts and instructions can easily be lost in the shuffle.

☐ Rickshaw-type, low-riding carts are available to pull more than one child with a single bicycle. Make sure they are attached properly and all children are harnessed in place while riding.

☐ Use bicycle paths or lightly traveled streets. Ride cautiously at a reduced speed.

☐ Drive on the right with traffic. Be aware of the causes of bicycle accidents:

- riding on the wrong side of the street
- not stopping for traffic signs and signals
- darting out of driveways and alleys
- riding without lights
- motorists turning left without yielding to an oncoming bicyclist or opening a car door in front of one

☐ Never allow tricycles or low-riding three-wheelers on the streets. Draw a red line to remind small children of the safe areas where they may ride.

☐ Use hand signals to indicate turning, and teach these signals to your young bicyclist.

☐ Keep all bicycles in good repair. Give them the bounce treatment to see if they appear shaky or any parts fall off.

☐ When your four- or five-year-old is ready to ride a two-wheel vehicle, your supervision and teaching will assure safe riding experiences. Never force a child who is not ready and willing to learn.

☐ Fit the bicycle properly with either 12-inch or 16-inch wheels. The bicycle that is too large or too small is both dangerous and uncomfortable. Get professional advice when purchasing the bicycle.

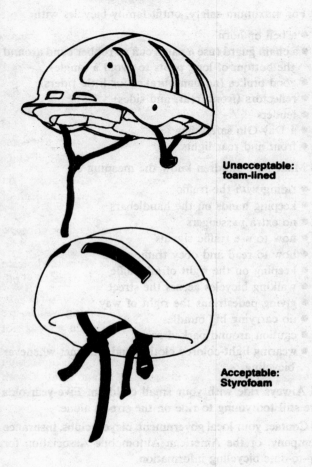

Bike Helmets

Unacceptable: foam-lined

Acceptable: Styrofoam

Foam-lined helmets may look comfortable and safe, but they do not provide enough protection to prevent serious injury. When shopping for bicycle headgear look for the hard Styrofoam variety.

☐ For maximum safety, outfit family bicycles with:

- a bell or horn
- a chain guard (use a pants cuff or rubber band around the bottom of long pants to avoid a tangle)
- good brakes (no hand brakes for little riders)
- reflectors (front, rear, and sides)
- fenders
- a Day-Glo safety flag
- front and rear lights

☐ Make sure children know the meaning of:

- riding *with* the traffic
- keeping hands on the handlebars
- no extra passengers
- how to use traffic signals
- how to read and obey traffic signs
- keeping on the right of all traffic
- walking bicycles across the street
- giving pedestrians the right of way
- no carrying big bundles
- caution around parked cars
- wearing light-colored clothes and a helmet whenever bicycling

☐ Always ride with your small children. Five-year-olds are still too young to ride on the streets alone.

☐ Contact your local government, bicycle clubs, insurance company, or the American Automobile Association for up-to-date bicycling information.

☐ Hand-me-down bicycles are always available. Consult a bicycle shop to make sure these bicycles are safe. The following safety checklist may help you identify any problems that need some attention:

- Is the seat tight?
- Is the chain too loose or damaged?
- Is there a bell or horn?
- Do the brakes work properly?
- Are reflectors adequate?
- Are handlebars tight?
- Are handgrips in place?
- Do tires have correct air pressure?
- Do pedals appear smooth or worn?
- Are tire valves capped?
- Are there any spokes bent, broken, or missing?

Family cycling can be a great way for all members of the family to let off some extra steam. Confidence on a bicycle is essential for small children to learn. Unfortunately, the tendency for us as adults is to gain a sometimes false sense of security when we see how well they are doing. Keep this in mind when you are tempted to send your young cyclist off on an independent mission before his sixth birthday. Above all, remember that head injuries can be prevented by wearing a good helmet. Adequate headgear is your family's greatest protection from serious harm.

A FINAL MESSAGE ABOUT TOYLAND

Toy safety is one of the most difficult areas of childproofing. It is an ever-changing part of our homes that cannot be taken care of through a simple home inspection and a few devices. Toys provide long hours of creative play, and we naturally hesitate to deprive our children of anything that seems fun, popular, and at the same time a learning tool. All we ask of you is all we ask of ourselves: Do your best to provide safe toy choices, stay educated on recalls and toy safety through the press, and report any toys that fall short of your expectations so that our collective voice is heard and unsafe toys are eliminated from store shelves.

Chapter Seven
Outdoor Safety

Your child's existence is not confined to the inside of your house. A great deal of her time is spent out of doors and because your responsibility for her safety extends to wherever she may find herself, there are certain additional precautions and safety measures you need to consider.

This chapter is divided into a number of checklists having to do with outdoor safety. These include: yard area safety, outdoor water safety, playground safety, and sun safety.

THE YARD AND OTHER AREAS NEAR THE HOME

FALLING OR TRIPPING HAZARDS

☐ Look for broken surfaces on sidewalks and stepping-stones. Make arrangements to have such tripping hazards repaired.

☐ Check porches and steps for loose boards and broken screens.

☐ Put rock salt on your walkways before the snowfall.

☐ Avoid grease and oil buildup in your driveway.

☐ Walk the lawn or surface area around your home and search for any holes, ditches, or ponds that need to be filled. This would be a good time to inspect for broken glass, cigarette butts, sharp objects, or obstacles for the lawn mower.

☐ Any window wells around basement windows should have barriers.

☐ Make sure there are no underground wells or shafts around your home.

☐ Screen any storm drains on your property. Write letters and make phone calls to public authorities regarding unsafe storm drains on public property.

☐ Determine the condition of your stairs. Hazardous railings? Dry rot or deterioration? Any openings that a child could fit her head into and become stuck?

☐ Inspect lawn furniture.

☐ Avoid any clotheslines that appear unsafe. Make sure excess cord is put up and out of the way.

☐ Check the condition of the trees in your yard. Have any dead trees or limbs removed.

☐ Remove any insect-infested woodpiles from your yard. Make sure the wood that you store is free of nails and is not used as a play area.

☐ Avoid leaving garden hoses lying around in the hot summer sun. Not only are they a tripping hazard, the water in the hose may become hot enough to scald.

GATES AND FENCES

☐ Fenced-in yards where children can play safely are a priority for many new families. Keep in mind that fences do not guarantee that a child will not wander into the street. Try to plan activities or reading that you can do outside while monitoring playtime.

☐ Check fences for peeling paint and splinters. Budget to have them repaired.

☐ Make sure gates have a lock too high for a two-year-old to open.

☐ Secure any loose boards. Also fill any holes that allow small children to slide under a fence.

THE TOOL SHED

☐ Organize a separate locked room for your tools.

☐ Know how to throw the main switch in case of an electrical emergency.

☐ Disconnect all power tools after each use. Do not use such tools around your baby.

☐ Store standing ladders in a horizontal position.

☐ Keep garden tools picked up, organized, and out of a child's reach. Hanging tools against a wall, head upward, is one way of keeping the area safe.

☐ Cover all electrical outlets with safety caps. Do this in all areas outside your home.

☐ Keep the tool shed off limits to children five and under.

LAWN MOWERS

☐ Teach children to stay clear of lawn mowing.

☐ Never mow while your baby is near. Flying debris is unavoidable.

☐ Lock the lawn mower in an area inaccessible to children and keep any ignition keys out of a child's reach.

POISON HAZARDS

Lead Poisoning

☐ Remove any loose house paint with a broom or stiff brush. Discard carefully.

☐ Always assume that old paint has at least one layer of lead-based paint. Keep this in mind if you own an older home.

☐ If you ever suspect your child has been eating bits of paint, call your poison control center.

Garden Poisons

☐ Determine the name of plants in your yard and tag them with the appropriate name.

☐ Check plant life against the poisonous plant Appendix. Clearly mark any poisonous yard plants and teach your children to avoid the danger.

☐ Inspect your yard regularly for seasonal surprises such as poisonous mushrooms, poison ivy, poison oak or sumac.

☐ Keep seeds and bulbs out of a child's reach.

☐ All fertilizers and pesticides must be kept under lock and key. Remind yourself to wash carefully any pails used to mix these toxins.

☐ Highly toxic chemicals are used to keep our lawns green. Have a professional tend your lawn for the next few years. Know what chemicals he applies to the lawn and when it will be safe for a small child to play on it.

Disposing of Toxic Pollutants

☐ Let paint dry out, or mix in sand or kitty litter before placing the can in a refuse container.

☐ To dispose of cooking oil and the like, pour it into containers stuffed with paper or kitty litter to soak up the oil.

☐ Take your waste motor oil (in clean, capped containers) during business hours to a service station participating in an oil recycling program.

☐ Never dump antifreeze in your yard or driveway because its sweetish taste is appealing to animals and its bright color may attract young children, who can be poisoned by tasting puddles of antifreeze.

☐ Believe it or not, decks, picnic tables, and outdoor furniture may pose a threat. Wood preservatives used to coat these areas are toxic substances. The three most common preservatives are creosote, inorganic arsenic compounds, and pentachlorophenol. Suspect items should be sealed with at least two coats of shellac or other sealant.

FIRE AND BURN HAZARDS

Flammable Substances

☐ Avoid the accumulation of old newspapers, cardboard cartons, and other flammable paper products.

☐ Keep oily rags in airtight metal containers.

☐ Keep flammable liquids tightly sealed. Store them away from any pilot light or other heat source.

The Backyard Barbecue

☐ Set up the barbecue clear of trees, shrubs, or other small timber.

☐ Use approved fire starters, not kerosene or gasoline.

☐ Keep a bucket of sand or water nearby to douse a flare-up.

☐ Use a portable area enclosure to surround the barbecue. By securing the grill on the inside you can keep your child and pets away from the hazard. The other option is to keep your child in an area enclosure or playpen while using a barbecue.

☐ Do not use a grill in an enclosed area such as a patio. Toxic fumes can build up.

☐ Avoid loose, dangling clothes while tending the fire.

☐ Make sure the fire is completely out before leaving. The fire is out when the coals are cool enough to pick up and dispose of properly.

DRIVEWAY SAFETY

☐ The best driveways are level, well-lit, and unobstructed on either side.

☐ Allow no playing in a parked car. Keep the car doors locked just in case.

☐ No firearms in the car.

☐ Teach children to stay clear of the driveway when a car is starting. Also request that small passengers be quiet while you back out of the driveway.

☐ Always back the car out slowly.

☐ Make a habit of walking around the back of the car

before entering the driver's seat and backing out. Check for balls, toys, sleeping animals, etc., on your trip around the car.

☐ When carrying the groceries in, take the baby in first, along with the ignition key.

☐ Beware of electric windows in cars. While parked, be sure to take the key out of the ignition.

☐ Stash flares, fire extinguishers, first-aid kits (and even the cigarette lighter if it is an attraction). Keep these items in a locked trunk or child-safe compartment in the car.

☐ Opt for battery-operated flashers instead of flares.

☐ Order childproof locks for the back doors of four-door cars.

RULES FOR YARD SAFETY

☐ Never allow a small child to leave the yard without permission.

☐ Determine what trees are safe for climbing. Never allow tree climbing without an adult nearby.

☐ No kites or model airplanes in the rain. Use them in a safe area free of electrical lines.

RULES FOR TRAFFIC SAFETY

☐ Teach your child never to run into the street. Use a ball rolling into the street to demonstrate the hazard.

☐ Make it a rule to hold hands while crossing the street.

☐ Teach small children about the colors and symbols used in traffic signals. Remember, your good example is most influential in showing how they are meant to work.

OUTDOOR WATER SAFETY

SWIMMING SAFETY

Some controversy exists about the ideal time to teach children how to swim. We suggest that you organize swim lessons for your children when they are around three years old. Avoid infant swim programs that advocate total submersion. Critics of infant swim classes feel that very small children gain a false sense of security. Parents agree that small children tend to become overconfident and let their guard down.

Water intoxication or hyponantremia is the condition that occurs when an infant swallows too much water. When swim programs encourage total submersion, this condition becomes a threat. Because of the higher risk of infection, water intoxication, and overconfidence in very young children, swim lessons after the third birthday make more sense.

Here are some additional rules of thumb to keep in mind:

☐ Never leave small children alone near a pool or on a beach.

☐ Floating devices such as rubber rings or water wings should always be worn by children who do not yet know how to swim.

☐ Test the water temperature before a swim. Warm water kept at about 80 degrees F. is most comfortable for early water experiences.

☐ Empty your store-bought wading pools and tubs after each use.

☐ Parents, lifeguards, or some designated supervisor

should always be monitoring water play. They should know how to summon emergency help and be trained in CPR and in swimming lifesaving techniques.

☐ Never let small children use inflatable toys or inner tubes as life preservers.

☐ No face masks or fins for children five and under.

☐ Clean all toys out of the pool or beach area after each use. Tragic accidents occur when little ones go for the floating ball or rubber ducky that was left abandoned in the water.

☐ When children are swimming, watch for signs of fatigue. Weakness, dizziness, chills, and a purplish hue around the lips and fingernails are all warning signs. Call for a rest break whenever you notice any of these signs.

POOL SAFETY CHECKLIST

☐ Treat pool chemicals like any other toxic substance: Keep them under lock and key.

☐ Do not use any electrical appliances near the pool.

☐ Make sure all pool areas are enclosed by a fence with a child-safe, lockable gate. Many local governments have specific fence requirements. In general, a fence that measures four to six feet high with a self-closing, self-latching gate should be sufficient. Make sure the fence cannot be climbed over or crawled under.

☐ Consider additional safety measures such as a padlock on the gate when the pool is not in use, and a commercial pool alarm.

☐ Check to see if any electrical outlets fail to have the GFCI (ground fault circuit interrupter) outlets. You will see a small reset button on the cover that will tip you off.

The GFCI will help prevent electrical shock and should be used especially around pool areas.

☐ Inspect pool ladders, steps, diving boards, slides, and handrails. Make sure they are mounted properly and securely. Check for broken parts, sharp edges, and loose bolts.

☐ Keep pools covered when not in use. Quickly remove any standing water that accumulates on the cover after a rainfall. A pool cover should be removed completely before anyone hops into the water.

☐ Inspect drains regularly. Make sure there are no broken or loose-fitting covers for children to tamper with.

☐ Keep the pool clean and clear of any slippery surfaces. Keep it filled properly and test the water regularly with a reliable test kit. Never add pool chemicals when swimmers are in the pool.

☐ Make sure a long pole and some form of flotation device are in the pool area.

☐ Teach small children the following rules:

- No running
- No glass in the pool area
- No pushing others into the water
- No swimming alone
- No swimming during a lightning storm
- No playing near drains, pumps, grates, or fittings of any kind.
- Keep long hair tied back.
- Swim only in supervised areas.
- No back dives in backyard pools.
- No diving off the side of the diving board.
- No diving except where permitted; the water depth must be at least five feet. Make sure your young

diver learns the importance of "steering up" after any headfirst entry.

- No diving should be permitted into an aboveground pool.

OTHER WATER HAZARDS

☐ Be sure your neighbor's pools, ponds, wells, or cisterns are not accessible to small children.

☐ With small children in mind, avoid playful water-wiggling hoses, and slippery water slides.

☐ Keep children away from hot tubs, spas, and Jacuzzis. Heated water and bubbling mechanisms can present additional risks.

☐ Avoid pool slides for children five and under. If you are confident that your five-year-old water bug is ready for the slide, make sure the rules are set and you are waiting nearby to lend a helping hand.

☐ Make it a rule: no alcohol consumption while monitoring your children in the water. Keep your mind clear and your wits about you.

BOATING

First-choice boating experience with small children ought to be at an amusement park or a ferry. If you must go boating with the family, remember the universal safety rules for all ages:

- Everybody must wear a life jacket. Look for the United States Coast Guard (USCG) approval label. The life preserver should have a Type I or II USCG approval. Make sure the size is appropriate for your child.

- Plan short trips. Children can easily become bored, restless, and fidgety in less than two hours.
- No rambunctious playing. Keep movement to a minimum.
- When boarding, pass a child to someone already on the boat.
- Avoid fastening a child to the boat. Seat belts are unnecessary.
- Keep children inside the boat, not sitting on the bow.
- Avoid speeding, sharp turns, shallow water, and busy boating areas. Go slow, relax, and enjoy the day.

PLAYGROUND SAFETY

Falls are the major accident occurring on the playground. The top three danger zones are slide ladders, monkey bars, and swings. The following checklist will help you make a safety evaluation of playgrounds in your neighborhood. If you find that your school or public playground fails to measure up to current safety standards, gather forces and approach your school board or city hall. You can make the difference!

☐ Never leave a child unattended at a playground (sitting in the car just will not do!) Observe park department employees or schoolyard attendants and decide for yourself whether or not they are actually supervising your children adequately. If not, stick around and enjoy it.

☐ Playground equipment should be installed over a soft surface. Wood chips, bark, and shredded tires are acceptable choices. Sand and grass or soil-covered areas are all right if maintained properly. Pea gravel is "soft," but a poor choice because small children tend to shove the pebbles in their mouths, ears and noses.

☐ Playground equipment should be installed at least six feet from any barrier such as a wall or fence.

☐ Check for hazardous equipment. The list includes:

- S-type hooks
- sharp edges
- splintered wood
- rings between 5 and 10 inches wide
- loose or exposed nuts and bolts (plastic caps are available as covers or you can stick on some fluorescent tape to at least show the hazard)
- unanchored equipment and concrete anchors that are not covered or cushioned
- wood, metal, or heavy plastic swing seats. Soft, long seats, tire swings, and canvas are acceptable choices.
- uncovered sandboxes. (Cats and other animals are inclined to use them as litter boxes, and their excretions sometimes contain parasites which could be harmful to your child.)
- trash or broken glass littering the grounds
- tripping hazards on the playground or field, including holes, sprinkler heads, tree stumps, or old cracked cement
- Twirling merry-go-rounds are generally taboo. A hazard exists if a space is worn between the ground and the bottom of the apparatus. If the space is greater than four inches, entrapment of body parts can accidentally occur. Careful monitoring is needed around the merry-go-round.

SUGGESTIONS FOR A PARENT'S ROLE IN PLAYGROUND SAFETY

☐ Make sure adequate safety inspections are scheduled for public, school, and backyard playgrounds. If maintenance seems poor, take steps to conduct your own neighborhood inspections and present reports at council meetings. Your efforts can bring the issue to light and motivate change.

☐ If some of the playground equipment seems too advanced for babies and toddlers, suggest separate equipment for different age groups and a posted color-code system. By color-coding equipment for different age groups, parents and supervisors can better monitor for safety.

☐ Be sure an adult can help stranded children on all pieces of playground equipment. Can you climb the slide, crawl into the jungle gym, or into the sandbox dome? You may need to extract an injured or frightened child from some tight spots on the playground.

☐ If swings or slides are particularly slippery, try gluing some nonslip bathtub strips onto the seat or bottom of the slide.

☐ Become aware of any hazards in the near vicinity of the playground. Are there any underground mine shafts? Uncovered storm drains? Empty houses? New construction sites? Dumps? Irrigation ditches? Keep these hazards in mind while your child grows, and set firm rules.

☐ If barbecue grills are in the area, make sure they are located away from dry grass. Parents can contribute to picnic safety by:

- not barbecuing in high winds or near softball games.
- never disposing of charcoal by dumping it on the ground.
- choosing self-starting charcoal that does not require lighter fluid.
- keeping toddlers in a safe area enclosure while grill is hot.

☐ Contact these playground safety experts for information and suggestions:

National Safety Council
School and College Department
444 N. Michigan Avenue
Chicago, IL 60611

Report complaints to:

U.S. Consumer Product Safety Commission
Washington, D.C. 20207

PLAYGROUND RULES

Children need to feel comfortable asking for help if they see a fight or accident on the playground. If you spend some time with your children setting rules and teaching safety, they will know how to identify an urgent situation and feel confident asking for help.

Parents, teachers, and recreation leaders all need to make sure children understand the importance of playground rules. Remember that in order for small children to learn and understand these rules, you must present a physical experience along with the verbal statement. For example, instead of just saying, "Don't walk in front of a moving swing," put on a theatrical performance. Place your child on the swing, give a little push, and walk in front and in back of her. Show how the child in the swing cannot stop and will end up hitting the bystander. Keep it light but serious, allowing your child to both hear and understand each rule. Scare tactics are not the answer for teaching safety lessons to small kids.

Here is a list of safety lessons to teach and rules to set:

Rules for Using the Slide

- No climbing the slide the wrong way.
- Hold on with both hands as you climb the steps of the slide. Climb one step at a time.
- Stay at least one arm's length from other children on the slide.
- Slide down feet first, one at a time.
- Make sure there are no children standing at the bottom of the slide.
- Be patient; no pushing or going in front of anyone in line.
- Leave the bottom of the slide after each turn.
- Don't use the slide if it feels too hot.

Rules for Using the Swings

- No twisting swings or swinging empty swings.
- No kneeling or standing on a moving swing.
- Sit in the center of the seat.
- Hold on to the swing with both hands.
- Stop completely before getting off.
- Be careful walking both in front and in back of a moving swing.
- No pushing.
- One person in a swing at a time.

Rules for Using Monkey Bars

- No climbing bars on a wet day.
- Use both hands.

- Be careful climbing down. Never jump from the top.
- Avoid too many kids on the bars at the same time.
- Watch out for the other kids coming down or swinging their feet.

Rules for Using the Seesaw

- Both children must get off together.
- Sit facing each other.
- Hold on with both hands.
- Never stand or walk across the board.
- Keep feet out from underneath the board as it descends.

Additional Rules

- Use playground equipment properly. No speed contests or acrobatics!
- No fighting or throwing sand or dirt.

You will be the motivating factor in developing safe playground behavior for your children. Keep your child's individual physical and emotional timetable in mind, and try not to push her into classes, playground activities, or structured team sports if she is not interested. A positive, loving approach will minimize your children's fears and provide an excellent outlet for all that extra energy.

SENSIBLE SUN SAFETY

☐ Be alert to the sun's intensity at certain times of the day. Between 10 A.M. and 2 P.M. (11 A.M. and 3 P.M. during Daylight Saving Time) the sun's rays are most intense.

☐ Some children are at a high risk for sun sensitivity. If your children have fair skin with blond or red hair and light eyes, be sure not to schedule outdoor activities for the peak sunshine time of day.

☐ Children need sunscreen too! If your children do spend time in the sun, apply sunscreen liberally and frequently.

☐ Infants should be kept out of direct sunlight as much as possible during their first year.

☐ Make sure that you cover up young children with long-sleeved shirts, long pants, and a hat if they are in direct sunlight for an extended length of time.

Sun safety cannot be taken lightly. Researchers note that a history of painful or blistering sunburns before the age of twenty can more than double the risk of developing skin cancer later in life. Make sun safety a priority.

Chapter Eight
Animals and Small Children

Domestic pets are a wonderful experience that help small children enjoy the wonders of life. Researchers have discovered that the sensory stimulation small children receive from playing with pets can actually help to facilitate learning. Research also has found that people who had pets as children seemed to have greater self-esteem. After all, they grew up with a "best friend" who was there no matter what, a therapeutic guru who listened when Mom and Dad were too busy.

Nonetheless, animals are living creatures, often unpredictable and capable of harming small children. Caution is recommended for families that already own pets, and a safety checklist follows for your review. For those considering a pet, a separate checklist is presented. We suggest you weigh the pros and cons carefully before taking on the added responsibility of a new member of the family. A final checklist on untamed animals lists additional safety measures to consider.

FAMILIES WITH PETS

☐ Never leave a baby alone in a room with a pet.

☐ Pay extra attention to your pet when your child is in the

room. All pets react differently when a new baby becomes part of the family.

☐ Continue your routine walks and games with your pet after the baby arrives. This will aid in a smooth transition.

☐ Do not allow any pet to sleep with your baby.

☐ Keep animal food dishes clean.

☐ Keep litter boxes out of reach and clean up dog droppings in yard areas where your children play.

☐ Control fleas! (Remember to do this chore alone. Flea collars, powders, and baths contain pesticides which can be harmful to small children.)

☐ Maintain up-to-date immunizations for your pets.

☐ Keep turtle bowls, fish tanks, birdcages, and rodent cages clean and out of your child's reach.

☐ Let your child start the feeding chores around four or five years old. Do not let the littler ones feed your pets.

☐ Be aware that there are many diseases associated with animals, including salmonella (from turtles); psittacosis (from birds); and ringworm, roundworm, Cheyletus mites, sarcoptic mange, rabies, and toxoplasmosis (from dogs and cats). All of these pet-related health problems can be prevented with good hygiene, regular veterinary visits, or vaccinations.

☐ Teach your children the following rules:

- Do not take toys or food away from a pet.
- Never grab an animal while it is asleep.
- Use caution around strange dogs: do not reach for them through a fence or grab them from behind.
- Do not tease or overexcite animals.
- Respect animals. ("Gentle" is an early buzzword to teach babies.)

- Do not interfere in an animal fight.
- Wash hands after playing with pets.

FAMILIES CONSIDERING PETS

So, you are considering a pet? Know the risks.

☐ Read through the "Families with Pets" checklist before you make a decision.

☐ Mention the idea to your pediatrician. Ask for advice. Often they can provide literature on the subject, especially regarding pets and allergies.

☐ Do any family members have allergies or asthma? (How about your baby-sitter?) Pets are not generally a good idea under these circumstances.

☐ Do you have enough time to take care of a pet? Feeding, walks, housebreaking, cleaning—it is no picnic! If the stress of an added responsibility outweighs the benefits of a pet, wait a few years.

☐ Make sure you have sufficient space for a pet.

☐ Consider the added noise level (especially from birds and dogs).

☐ Can you afford it? Smaller pets usually cost less to care for.

☐ Do you travel frequently? Consider the arrangements you will need to make for family vacations and other overnight trips.

UNTAMED OUTDOOR LIFE

Insect stings and wild animal bites can be fatal. Preventive action can decrease the risk while allowing you to enjoy the out-of-doors.

☐ Veto the idea of wild animals such as fox cubs, monkeys, and snakes as household pets for small children.

☐ Wild animals are unpredictable. Keep your car windows rolled up while touring a wildlife park. Refrain from feeding wild animals (even the squirrels) at the zoo.

☐ Animals can be carriers of rabies.

- Avoid any animal that appears to be acting strangely.
- Rabid animals can attack without provocation. They are often thirsty, appear agitated, and may foam at the mouth.
- Report any suspicious animal to your local government health authority.

☐ If your child is bitten by an animal, do not panic. Identify the animal and, with help, attempt to detain it for an examination. You will need to know that the animal is not rabid. Wash the wound with soap and water and seek immediate medical attention.

☐ Take action to prevent insect stings and bites.

- Require shoes to be worn outdoors.
- Keep children out of bushes, vines, and other known nesting areas.
- Warn children not to touch or tease insects. Remember, they learn by your example.
- Avoid apple juice and other sweet food and drink on picnics.

Chapter Nine
Parent as Safety Device

What exactly do we mean by "parent as safety device"? Basically, that by preparing yourself, your home, and your family; by arming yourself with knowledge and putting into practice what you know about child development and devices; and by teaching safety to your children and changing certain habits that may be detrimental to your child's safety, you will be the best defense against potential home accidents. Just as that piece of hardware can intervene in potential child accident scenarios, so can an educated parent intervene on her child's behalf.

It seems like an enormous responsibility. Parenthood is. But the safety lessons and habits you impart to your children are good not only for them: you can reap the benefits as well. For instance, did you ever come home late at night and trip on the tennis shoe you left on the stairs? Readjusting your habits for the sake of your child may seem a bit inconvenient at first. It is just a question of retraining yourself to think in a more careful vein. And watching your child grow up happy and healthy is its own reward.

Below is a list of seemingly harmless habits characteristic of almost any parent. Each one carries the potential to threaten your child's safety in some way. Think about them. They are easy to change—for safety's sake.

HABITS TO BREAK

☐ Emptying your pockets and leaving small items that present a choking hazard within reach (for example, loose change).

☐ Leaving drawers open. Not only can they pinch little fingers, but they could contain items not suitable for them to play with.

☐ Leaving doors open that should remain closed, such as office, attic, garage, bathroom.

☐ Placing cleansers and other household chemicals within reach while using them.

☐ Failing to return medication to their safe storage area.

☐ Not lowering the toilet lid after use.

☐ Leaving smoking materials such as matches, lighters, and cigarettes, within a child's reach.

☐ Not properly disposing of razor blades, open tin cans, or other such items with sharp, cutting edges.

☐ Leaving the ironing board in the raised position and not storing the iron immediately after use.

☐ Keeping the stair areas cluttered with toys, shoes, and other items that will go up "the next time someone goes upstairs."

☐ Keeping your kitchen footstool (if you use one) accessible to your child. There are several brands on the market that are collapsible and easily stored in the broom closet. Opt for this type rather than one that must be left out all the time.

☐ Leaving your handbag within reach. There is nothing suitable for child's play in your handbag.

☐ Ignoring broken toys. You need to hold periodic toy checks. Broken, nonrepairable toys should be promptly disposed of. (See Chapter 6.)

☐ Not effectively using any safety devices you may have installed, for example, leaving a safety gate open after you have passed through.

☐ Not using your seat belt. Your child is more likely to resist being restrained in the car if she knows you do not abide by the same rules.

☐ Failing to dispose of dry cleaning bags properly.

☐ Failing to store garbage cans properly when not in use.

☐ Not watching children bathing in the tub.

☐ Failing to keep the bathroom free of toxins such as cosmetics and cleansers, to keep the bathtub edges free of shampoo, razors, etc., and to unplug hair dryers and electric razors when not in use.

☐ Not keeping the gate closed when the children are playing in the yard.

☐ Failing to keep a sandbox covered when not in use.

☐ Forgetting to unplug small electric appliances when not in use.

☐ Monogramming your child's clothing. This is not a sound idea: it could lead to potential problems with strangers addressing your child by name.

☐ Giving your child foods that could cause choking without making sure they are cut into manageable pieces. Get into the habit of making sure all food is adequately cut up. Among the most hazardous foods are hot dogs, hard candy, nuts, popcorn, peanut butter, and raw carrots.

☐ Tying pacifiers, toys, or food around your child's neck. This is a major choking hazard.

☐ Neglecting the proper storage of firearms and other weapons kept in the house.

☐ Not replacing sharp objects such as knives, scissors, razors, immediately after use.

HABITS TO CULTIVATE

☐ Find out if any of your house plants are toxic. Many times we are given plants as gifts. You need to be aware of which plants could harm your child if ingested. (See Appendix 1.)

☐ Keep track of when your child's immunizations and well-baby visits are due.

☐ Report unsafe toys, furniture, and baby equipment.

☐ Be cautious while drinking a hot beverage. Cups should be kept well out of reach and care taken while actually drinking.

☐ Cue guests as to your safety habits. Not explaining your safety procedures to visitors can lead to accidents. Do not be afraid to remind them to close the bathroom door behind them!

☐ Your child should be fingerprinted and photographed every six months; every three months under the age of two.

☐ Children should be encouraged to sit down for all snacks and meals. You can help foster this habit by adopting it yourself.

☐ When bringing toxins such as cleansers into the house, make it a habit to affix poison stickers to the containers immediately.

☐ Make it a habit to clean up after yourself. After any activity, items used should be returned to their storage area.

PREPARING FOR EMERGENCIES

When it comes to protecting your child from accidents, your habits are not the only factor to examine. The following checklists touch on situations which may never affect your child but which help to complete your preparedness. They include tips on fire safety, emergency education and how to prepare for handling a traumatic situation, and assembling a first-aid kit.

FIRE SAFETY

Preparing your family for this kind of emergency could save lives. There are several tips to consider.

☐ Plan not one, but two fire escape routes. Post them so that sitters and guests in your home will be aware of them, perhaps on the door of a hall closet.

☐ Have a periodic fire drill. Gather the family and practice leaving your house as mapped out on your fire escape route.

☐ Check smoke alarms frequently, especially those that are battery-operated.

☐ Make sure all fires in your fireplace are completely extinguished before you retire for the evening.

☐ Have your chimney swept periodically. This safety practice is often neglected.

EMERGENCY EDUCATION

How can you prepare yourself for emergency situations that might occur?

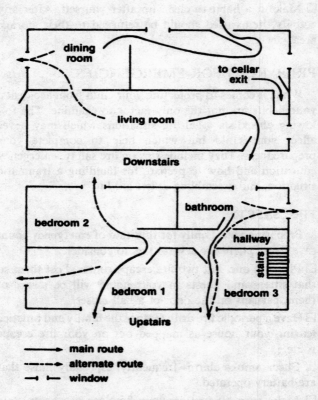

Fire Escape Routes

dining room

to cellar exit

living room

Downstairs

bedroom 2

bathroom

hallway

stairs

bedroom 1

bedroom 3

Upstairs

→ main route
–·–·→ alternate route
⊢––⊣ window

Make sure you plan two fire escape routes from each room in your home. Post your map where baby-sitters can easily find it.

☐ Enroll in a CPR class. Not only will you learn the technique that is responsible for saving thousands of lives of both adults and children, but you will be taught the Heimlich maneuver to assist a choking victim.

☐ Enroll in a first-aid class. They are offered through a number of organizations, among them the Red Cross and hospital education programs. These classes can run the gamut from the most basic to the more advanced.

☐ Enroll in a childproofing class. Your local hospital may offer such a class, or know where you can find one. CPR and first-aid instruction are often part of such programs.

☐ A number of helpful books are available to help you in traumatic situations. Among them:

A Sigh of Relief: The First-Aid Handbook for Childhood Emergencies by G. I. Green (Bantam Books, 1977). This book offers step-by-step illustrations for quick reference.

Emergency First-Aid for Children by E. B. Chewning (Addison-Wesley, 1984). This is a very simple, straightforward paperback.

PARENT'S FIRST-AID KIT

It is a good idea to put together an emergency first-aid kit to help with any minor medical emergencies either in the home or away. Many of these items can be found in camping stores. In it you should include:

- a plastic bag full of cotton balls or cosmetic cotton pads
- first-aid adhesive tape
- adhesive bandages in various sizes. (Specially designed strips with colorful stars and hearts come in handy.)
- steri-strip butterfly bandages

- a plastic bag full of cotton-tipped swabs. (Plastic bags that "zip" to seal are convenient.)
- some individually wrapped gauze squares in various sizes (2-inch squares and 4-inch squares)
- a roll of 2-inch wide gauze bandage
- a small pocketknife equipped with sharp scissors and tweezers
- a skin-sensitive thermometer
- child-designed measuring spoon and/or syringe
- elastic bandage
- a large bright bandana (useful as a sling or flag)
- acetaminophen (liquid and tablets)*
- syrup of ipecac
- activated charcoal
- petroleum jelly or lip lubricant
- a plastic bag full of isopropyl alcohol packets
- antibiotic ointment such as Neosporin
- analgesic eardrops (if your children are prone to ear infections)
- antacid tablets
- hydrocortisone cream
- sock (for ice) with a face drawn on it and some cold packs
- small bar of soap
- waterproof matches
- small flashlight
- quarter and a calling-card number
- reflective thermal space blanket (very small and looks like a foil sheet)

* Note: There is a proven correlation between the ingestion of aspirin to minimize flu symptoms in children and the disease Reyes syndrome. Use acetaminophen products from the start.

- a small emergency first-aid index. These are often available at your local hospital.
- a note describing family blood types and any allergies
- medical insurance numbers for each family member
- a whistle
- a few diaper pins
- any special medications

Believe it or not, all of this should fit into a locking fishing tackle box or similar file box. It will be perfect on the family camping trip or as a traveling first-aid kit in the car. Have it on hand for the baby-sitter or grandparents if you decide to go away for a weekend trip without the kids. If you have a vacation home, make a spare kit to leave there year-round.

TEACHING YOUR CHILD ABOUT ACCIDENT PREVENTION

Lessons regarding safety can be initiated almost from birth. Language is absorbed. As children grow, lessons can become more complex.

- Use words like "danger," "off limits," and the obvious "no" to indicate a potentially harmful situation.

- The word "hot" should be taught very early on. Every time you are cooking, or steam rises from a beverage or faucet, or you are lighting a fire or candles, indicate the possible danger by saying "hot!"

- Poison stickers are a marvelous teaching tool. These stickers may be obtained from your local poison control center for a nominal charge or purchased in the safety device section of your local stores. Affix them to all toxins in the house and remember to use them when you bring new substances into the home. Children quickly learn to recognize a cross-looking face.

● Teach your child to keep one hand on the car when it is parked in a lot until an adult can help them safely out of the traffic area. Children have a tendency to dash out of a parked car without realizing there are vehicles in motion everywhere.

Children need to have very basic rules regarding their behavior in relation to safety. Nobody wants to inhibit children, but we do need and want to protect them. As a parent you need to make choices regarding what you feel is appropriate behavior for your child. Set down guidelines and follow them closely. Rules that are consistently enforced are not so easily broken.

DAY-CARE SAFETY

Ensuring that your child is cared for in a safe, loving environment is an important priority and should be well researched. A day-care center must suit not only your needs, but your child's as well. A majority of your child's waking hours may well be spent in day care and you should be prepared to ask the right questions, so you know exactly where and how your child will be living when not safe at home with you.

Here are some points to consider when choosing a day-care facility:

THE MANAGEMENT

☐ Plan a visit to the facility you are interested in. Give yourself enough time to familiarize yourself thoroughly with the caregivers and the surroundings. This is true of both day-care centers and family day care.

☐ Is the facility licensed/registered by the state or any other agency?

☐ Are you made aware of all management policies regarding fees, hours, meals, vacations, illness, disciplinary methods, and activities schedules?

☐ Are you welcome to drop in and visit your child when you desire?

☐ Do you receive periodic reports on your child's progress?

THE ORGANIZATION

☐ Does the size of the group assigned to each caregiver allow for enough individual attention? The ratios should be as follows:

- family day care: 1 adult to 5 children
- day-care center: 1 adult to 3 to 4 infants; 1 adult to 4 to 6 two-year-olds; 1 adult to 7 to 8 three-year-olds; 1 adult to 8 to 9 four-year-olds; and 1 adult to 8 to 10 five-year-olds.

☐ Are there suitable substitutes available in case the primary caregiver is absent?

☐ Is the indoor space adequate for the needs of all the children?

☐ Is it well organized?

☐ Are there rest areas available with carpeting and comfortable chairs?

☐ Is there a safe outdoor play area?

☐ Are the children well supervised at all times?

☐ Are the children made well aware of the rules governing play both indoors and out?

THE CAREGIVERS

☐ Are they warm, affectionate, and energetic?

☐ Do they appear to be in good health?

☐ Are they prepared with good references and a background check if required by the state?

☐ Do they use a pleasant tone of voice when speaking with the children?

☐ Do they seem patient and happy to be around children?

☐ Do they have any child care-related training and/or do they keep up by reading or belonging to a professional organization?

☐ Will they discuss potential behavior problems with the parents?

☐ Do they maintain proper discipline through close supervision? There should be a policy of no spanking, shouting, verbal abuse, or withholding food as a means of punishment.

SAFETY

☐ Are electrical outlet caps, safety gates, and/or other devices in use?

☐ Are all toxins (cleaning fluids, etc.) kept well out of a child's reach?

☐ Are emergency phone numbers posted near the telephone?

☐ Are there an adequate number of smoke alarms and fire extinguishers in the building?

☐ Is there a planned fire escape route? Are there periodic drills?

☐ Is the outdoor play area fenced in and cleared of poisonous plants and debris? Does the sandbox have a cover when not in use?

HEALTH AND NUTRITION POLICIES

☐ Is the facility clean?

☐ Are phone numbers for both parents available in the event of a medical emergency? Is there a backup phone number?

☐ Are you apprised of any injury sustained by your child?

☐ Are caregivers responsible for washing their hands each time a child is taken to the toilet or a diaper is changed and before meals are served?

☐ Is there at least one caregiver trained in CPR and/or first aid?

☐ Are meals and snacks wholesome and nutritious?

☐ Are weekly menus provided to parents?

☐ Are babies held while being bottle-fed?

☐ Is there a naptime set aside with adequate beds/cots/mats, etc.?

☐ Is an emergency medical authorization letter available? A sample letter follows. Make sure to have it notarized.

TOY/PLAY SAFETY

☐ Are toys well organized and easy to locate?

☐ Are there adequate toys for each age group?

☐ Is there proper storage for toys which may not be appropriate for younger age groups?

☐ Are there colorful pictures on the walls at a child's eye level? Is the children's artwork displayed regularly?

CHILD'S EMERGENCY MEDICAL AUTHORIZATION

Name of Child
Birthdate
Name of Parents or other responsible adult
Home Address
Telephone #
Mother's Business Address
Telephone #
Father's Business Address
Telephone #

    The parent/guardian authorizes _____ [day-care provider] to obtain immediate medical care and consents to the hospitalization of, the performance of necessary diagnostic tests upon, the use of surgery upon, and/or the administration of drugs to, his/her child or ward if any emergency occurs when he/she cannot be located immediately.

    If parents cannot be reached, contact
Name
Address
Telephone #

Child's insurance #_____   Physician _____
                                      Telephone #_____

Date: _____   Parent's Signature _____

This form should be kept by the provider and taken to the medical facility in the event of an emergency. Have the completed form notarized to avoid any disputes in the emergency room.

☐ Are music, art materials, sand and water toys, and dress-up clothes available?

SOME SIGNS OF POOR CHILD CARE

☐ After several months your child shows signs of continued unhappiness or lapses into unhappiness after being seemingly adjusted.

☐ Your child's apparent fear of a caregiver.

☐ Frequent staff changes.

☐ Not allowing parents to drop by at any time during the day.

☐ Care that seems indifferent. Children are left to play alone for long periods of time; the caregiver is unable to answer the questions you have regarding your child's day.

Remember, as a parent you must trust your instincts. If you suspect there are problems with the facility you have chosen for your child, talk to other parents. Do they share your concerns? Discuss what your children are telling you individually. Keep informed.

PREPARING THE BABY-SITTER

Let's face it. At some point you are going to have to leave the house without your child and diaper bag in tow. Chances are you will be leaving your child with a sitter. Here are some things to consider when choosing one:

☐ Request references, preferably from someone you know.

☐ Be sure as to the hours the sitter is available and the fee charged.

☐ Does the sitter know how to handle various child care situations: diapering, toileting, bathing, feeding, etc.?

☐ Does the sitter know how to handle minor first-aid emergencies?

☐ Does the sitter seem to be a mature person who shows good judgment and understands the potential danger a child could get into?

You can help your sitter be comfortable in your home with your children if you take the time to explain the safety measures you have adopted for your family.

☐ Remember to post an emergency phone list (see example) next to each phone. Alongside keep:

- the address and phone number of where you will be
- the names of those you will be visiting
- your time schedule should you find yourself at more than one location during your outing

☐ Make sure your sitter knows where the fire escape routes are posted and walk her through the route if necessary.

☐ Indicate where all your child's medications are located; when and how they should be administered.

☐ Be sure to let the sitter know if any areas of the house such as the attic, den, or workshop are off limits.

☐ Point out the various safety devices around the house and how to use them.

☐ Make sure you have an emergency first-aid book available in the event of an accident.

☐ Provide a letter authorizing emergency medical treatment. (See sample letter.)

EMERGENCY PHONE LIST

WORK PHONE: Mom:

                  Dad:

CLOSE NEIGHBORS:

NEAREST FRIEND/RELATIVE:

DOCTOR: Name:

        Phone:

        Advice/After-hours advice:

INSURANCE I.D. #:

ALLERGIES & SPECIAL MEDICAL CONDITIONS:

TAXI:

POISON CONTROL CENTER:

LOCATION OF POISON ANTIDOTES:

        Syrup of Ipecac:

        Activated Charcoal:

ALL-NIGHT DRUGSTORE:

        Phone:

        Address:

HOSPITAL:

EMERGENCY MEDICAL SERVICES PHONE:

HOME ADDRESS:

HOME PHONE:

WHEN TALKING TO EMERGENCY PERSONNEL

1. Tell what happened.
2. To whom it happened.
3. How many people are involved.
4. What is being done.
5. You hang up last.

Chapter Ten

Out and About Safely with Children

Every parent at some point will have to face the possibility of traveling with a small child either by plane, train, bus, or car. The prospect of being confined in a small space with your child for hours on end can be terrifying, but it is one you can prepare for. A child's short attention span can threaten parental sanity and you need to face the challenge by pooling all your resources and not letting your child utter those fateful words "I'm bored" even once. A child who is kept safely occupied will not be able to get into trouble.

TRAVELING BY CAR

Getting into the car with your children, whether it be for a two-mile trip to the grocery store or a cross-country trip to see Grandma, can be difficult. How can we expect normal, healthy children to keep from fidgeting and fussing in the confinement of the back seat? The following list suggests ways to make everyone safer and more comfortable during these necessary voyages. An alert driver is much better able to anticipate and react to potential problems on the road which may interfere with the safety of everyone in the car. An occupied child is less likely to scream in your ear at the wrong moment and break your concentration.

The above drawing illustrates the correct method of securing three children in a back seat with only two seat belts.

□ All children should be secured inside the car at all times. Children under 40 pounds or four years of age should be seated in a government-approved car seat. The label on the car seat should state that the device meets Motor Vehicle Safety Standard No. 213. Older children should wear seat belts. Remember that portable cribs and/or car beds are considered unsafe and should never be used to transport children. Never allow your child to ride unfastened in the lap of another passenger. This could prove tragic in the event of a collision.

□ Parents and other adult passengers can encourage the use of car seats and safety belts by setting a good example. Children almost always want to copy the grown-ups; show them something safe to copy.

□ If good habits are initiated early and never varied, the

likelihood of your child's being bothered by the use of car seats or seat belts is greatly reduced.

☐ Grandparents may prove to be difficult in this area. After all, most of their generation never used them and their children survived. This is unacceptable. They and their children were lucky. The risk is not worth it. Be firm by insisting they strap your child in an approved car seat whenever traveling in a car. They'll learn by example too, so take the opportunity to be their best role model. A thoughtful way to approach the subject with them is by presenting them with their own car seat for their grandchild's special visits.

☐ To protect the upholstery under the car seat, consider using a piece of heavy vinyl carpet runner or carpet squares (manufacturer's discontinued samples), which can be obtained from carpet stores either free or for a nominal charge.

☐ In order to protect your child from extreme temperatures which may affect the car seat, remember always to keep it covered. Newborns especially must not be subjected to the burning vinyl of a seat that has been sitting for hours in a hot car. A blanket or towel thrown over the seat will shield it from summer heat and winter cold. Tailored car-seat covers will also provide the necessary protection on most car seats. Regardless of how you solve the problem, be mindful of the metal framework and other potential hot spots that may be exposed.

☐ Try to choose a car seat that allows the child to look out the window. If he can see what is going on outside of the car, he will be less tempted to get out of it for a better look.

☐ Remember to keep all heavy or sharp objects out of the passenger area. They should be placed securely in the trunk. The same holds true for objects on the dashboard or back shelf. A sudden stop may cause these objects to fly and injure someone.

☐ Keep the car well ventilated. Avoid smoking. Small children can be very sensitive to strong odors. Parents can easily avoid motion sickness problems by keeping the car temperature comfortable and clean air circulating.

☐ Try to avoid driving during peak stress times, in rush hour or vacation traffic jams. Everyone's patience wears thin at these times and you do not want to have to deal with your child's impatience as well. Also, try to avoid driving when you are angry, ill, or in a bad mood. You may make more mistakes in judgment.

☐ For longer trips, make sure you schedule frequent stops. It will give the kids a chance to romp around, have a snack, and breathe some fresh air.

☐ Also, for longer trips, consider traveling at night or early in the morning so the children will sleep.

☐ If hysteria breaks out, pull over and stop rather than pulling your child out of the car seat while the car is moving.

☐ Some nevers for you to remember:

- Never allow the child to play with car controls.
- Never leave the child in the car while you run an errand, even a short one.
- Never leave the motor running in or around an area where there may be children playing.
- Never leave a child in a running car in a garage. There is always the danger of carbon monoxide poisoning.
- Never allow children to eat lollipops or other hazardous foods in a moving vehicle.

- Never allow children to play with sharp objects such as pens or pencils.
- Never allow your child to ride on a passenger's lap, even with a seat belt around both.

KEEPING CHILDREN OCCUPIED IN THE CAR

Younger Children

- Sing their favorite songs. You may have to repeat them fifty times or more during a simple excursion, but it beats tears and uncontrollable commotion.
- Attach safe toys, rattles, and pacifiers to the car seat to provide easy access. (Remember the 12-inch rule: no strings longer than 12 inches, to avoid tangles and tragedy.) Many parents are now opting for brightly colored plastic chains to fasten toys to the car seat rather than string or ribbon which could tangle between little fingers.
- Turn on the radio.
- Keep an emergency basket on hand containing clean diapers, wipes, change of clothes, juice/formula, dry crackers, and whatever else suits your needs.

Older Children

- Books are always a good choice for the older child. They can help reduce the frequency of "Are we there yet?" Choose picture books and books with large print to avoid motion sickness.
- Bring along a tape recorder and favorite tapes if you do not have a cassette deck in your car. Story tapes are a wonderful diversion. There are a wide variety available on the market, with something to please every child's

taste. If you are organized, borrow some books from the library, read the stories on tape, and save the cassette and books for the long car trip. Children find it very soothing to have Mom or Dad telling the story, especially if they are not there for the trip.

● Try games like "I Spy," "Twenty Questions," "License Plate," or "I see an A,B,C . . ."

● There are a number of car travel games available commercially. Large toy-store chains usually keep a good selection in stock. Most involve keeping track of landmarks and are suitable for even preschoolers.

One last word about safety belts. You may on occasion find yourself with more children in the back seat than you have safety belts for. If that is the case, the simple diagram on page 187 will illustrate the safest way to secure your little passenger. Belts should fit snugly across the hips, not stomach. If the child must use a shoulder strap, make sure it does not come in contact with the child's neck or face; put it behind the child's head. Behind the seat is also an acceptable arrangement.

AIR TRAVEL

Here are some suggestions to help ensure that your airplane trip goes smoothly:

☐ Make reservations early in order to get a convenient flight. Off-peak hours are best, as you increase your chances of getting a vacant seat either for your toddler or as extra room for an older child.

☐ Request early seat selection. Aisles are convenient if you anticipate frequent walks and trips to the rest room. Bulkhead seats (wall in front) may also help in that there is extra floor space and no seats in front to be kicked with toys and squirming feet. The other passengers may be grateful to you for choosing the bulkhead.

☐ Airports are notoriously busy places. If children become separated from their parents it is very easy to lose them in the crowd. This may be the ideal spot for use of a harness of some type. With the older child, if holding hands is not possible get him used to holding the bottom of your jacket or sleeve. You will notice if that little "tug" loosens.

☐ During takeoff, secure older children properly and hold younger children on your lap with the safety belt around your hips only, not around the child. Several car seats are approved for air travel as well. If your arrangements permit, carry on the car seat and rest comfortably knowing you have provided the safest ride for your baby. For children under two, this may mean purchasing an additional ticket to guarantee this ideal situation.

☐ It is a good idea to have the children sucking on something to help counteract the effect of the change of air pressure on the ears, especially on landing. Give older children gum or candy; a filled bottle for the younger ones is best. Nursing is a great comfort for infants. If you arrive unprepared, do not hesitate to ask the flight attendant for a can of juice before takeoff.

☐ On a long, crowded flight while seated on an aisle seat, remember to keep your child's hands, feet, and head tucked in while you both nap. Flight attendants with carts or restless passengers push through in a hurry and may accidentally pinch a sleeping baby.

☐ If you need to rent a car at your destination, make arrangements ahead of time with the rental company.

Did you remember to bring everything with you? Here is a list of things to remember to throw into the diaper bag or flight bag. A good rule of thumb is to take everything you need for the children over a twenty-four-hour period in case your luggage takes a separate vacation.

☐ Bottles: the airlines generally provide juice and milk upon request, so there is no need to fill up with liquids from home. Ask for extras before deplaning. It may save you the bother of having to find a cafeteria.

☐ Favorite foods: things that are not too messy and require little preparation. Possibilities include pieces of fruit, cereal that is easily grasped in little fingers, perhaps candy. When your child is running out of control, you may be glad to be carrying a chocolate bar.

☐ Cleaning supplies: fresh diapers (the disposable variety are best for traveling), wipes, a wet washcloth in a plastic bag for big messes, tissues, lotion, and powder. Add a change of clothes.

☐ Small toys that have proved to keep your child happy at home will work best in the air. Now is not a good time to experiment with the new rattle your child received for Christmas. Bring toys that you *know* will interest your child. Inflatable toys are a good choice since they are easy to pack and to assemble.

☐ If all of the above fail to keep your child happy, a walk to the rest room is sure to please him. Fill up the sink, take off his shoes and socks and let him splash around a bit. You would be surprised how quickly time will pass when you are occupied in this way.

☐ Travel with a pack or lightweight stroller. You can take them on board with you and they can be a lifesaver when carting a sleepy child through a crowded airport.

☐ Keep in your carry-on bag a coin purse for emergency phone calls. Any emergency medical information should be tucked in your bag somewhere with a medical insurance number, names, home address and phone number. If your child is on medication, keep it in your carry-on baggage just in case your checked bags get lost.

A WORD ABOUT OLDER CHILDREN

Air travel generally means a change in routine. Changes in routine can cause upsets. A way to avoid this is to involve your child in the travel plans. Talk to him about what will happen; read stories together about air travel; allow him to pack his own flight bag (you can go through it later and remove the twenty-pound battery-operated model jet); let him know this is fun. Your enthusiasm will rub off on him.

For older children consider bringing:

● Favorite foods: airplane fare does not have much appeal for adults, let alone children. Indulge their need for a treat and balance it with fruit, nuts, a peanut butter and jelly sandwich, or yogurt.

● Cleanup supplies: a change of clothes, washcloth, toothbrush, tissues, etc.

● Toys: new coloring books or workbooks, crayons, felt pens and paper, action figures, stickers. Think small and compact. You will end up carrying most of this stuff when little arms get tired. Try packing it all in a small backpack and make him responsible for carrying something too.

● Sometimes buying a small gift and presenting it on the airplane helps short-circuit a child's impatience.

Upon arriving at your destination, understand that your child is in new, unfamiliar surroundings. Provide lots of love and reassurance.

TRAIN TRAVEL

Train travel is less popular than in the past, but still a possibility. If you are planning a train trip, follow the guidelines for air travel with these additions:

☐ Bring along your car seat with an extra-long belt to secure it to the train seat.

☐ Trains are drafty. Bring along an extra sweater or a lightweight sleeping bag for naptime.

☐ If you are traveling for a few days and find yourself loaded with a lot of carry-on luggage, bring a small extra bag that you can take along wherever you move on the train.

☐ Avoid leaving children unattended with strangers when you go to the rest room. Baby backpacks or front carriers work well for moving small children on the train.

☐ Dress small children in comfortable, brightly colored clothing. They will be much easier to spot if they wander off.

TRAVEL TO FOREIGN COUNTRIES

Challenging adventure awaits those who must travel abroad. The best advice we can offer is to plan ahead carefully and remember the following:

☐ Contact your pediatrician regarding possible immunizations.

☐ Contact the American Embassy in the country(ies) you will be visiting and try to obtain the name of a reputable English-speaking pediatrician, just in case.

☐ Bring all medication that you may require, including painkillers, fever reducers, diaper rash ointments, sunscreens, syrup of ipecac, and a traveling first-aid kit. Books are available to help make these preparations (see Appendix 4).

☐ Bring a front carrier, backpack, or umbrella stroller, whichever suits your specific needs.

☐ Bring a favorite blanket or other security object.

☐ Teach your child a couple of foreign language phrases such as "My name is . . . ," or "I am lost."

☐ Make sure your child knows the name of the hotel at which you are staying. As an added precaution, put a note in your child's pocket which reads, "I am staying at . . ." and the name of your hotel.

☐ Check with your health insurance company to see if you have any coverage for overseas medical costs.

VISITING A RELATIVE'S HOME

It is not always easy to make childproofing recommendations or requirements known to a relative you may be visiting. When the right moment occurs, be sure to make your host aware of your needs as diplomatically as possible. Before planning a trip to visit your child's grandmother, for instance, why not write or call ahead and offer a few suggestions to help everyone feel more comfortable when your child visits.

Ask relatives to:

☐ Remove all medication and toxic cleaning materials from within child's reach.

☐ Move all breakables from low to high locations.

☐ Remove all toxic plants (you may want to send a list from your poison control center).

☐ Make sure they have safe, adequate equipment such as a high chair, crib, car seat, etc. Renting is cheaper than purchasing and can be done fairly easily.

☐ Consider taking along a traveling safety kit containing useful, easily transported and installed devices to help secure the home you are visiting. Include in your kit:

- 15 electrical outlet caps
- syrup of ipecac/activated charcoal
- basic medications or entire first-aid kit
- poison stickers
- doorknob cover
- night light

SHOPPING WITH YOUR CHILD

What is it about a store aisle that makes a two-year-old want to imitate a Boeing 747? Even a child who has been sound asleep in the car is revived by the sight of aisles! So what is the harm, you say? How much trouble can they get into? Plenty.

Losing a child in a store is a traumatic event for everyone. The stress that accompanies it is great and can upset your whole day. Take heart. The following suggestions may prevent trouble.

FOR YOUNGER CHILDREN:

☐ Try to plan you outings when your child is most likely to nap (but not after 4 P.M.)

☐ Strollers are ideal for shopping trips. Or consider using a backpack or front carrier to keep your hands free.

☐ For supermarket excursions bring along your own safety strap for use in the grocery cart. Some stores are now outfitting their carts with safety straps. For infants, consider using an infant seat or purchasing one of the commercial products designed to keep your child safe in the seat portion of the grocery cart. There are some car seats that can easily be transported into the shopping cart as well.

☐ Bring along a bottle, rattle, teething biscuit, or other safe toy.

☐ Carry with you a well-stocked diaper bag. You may want to leave this bag in the car if you do not mind a jog back to the car if the need arises.

☐ Try to shop when everyone has a full stomach. Both you and your child will last longer.

FOR OLDER CHILDREN:

☐ Try to plan your shopping excursions when children are the least fatigued, usually in the morning.

☐ Dress your children in brightly colored clothing. They will be easier to spot should they become separated from you.

☐ Bring along a simple snack. When they are tired, find a quiet place and let them refuel. Portable juice boxes are often a welcome treat along with a granola bar or box of raisins.

☐ Exercise patience. If they say they are tired, let them sit down for a breather and then continue.

☐ If you are in a mall where there is a toy store, promise a short visit "to look at the toys" if they behave until you are through with your shopping.

☐ Try not to let them wander from your side. Avoid the expense of any kind of electronic beeper device. They tend to allow us to let our guard down.

☐ Use caution in allowing your child to ride on electric-operated rides outside supermarkets and drugstores. Many of these rides are poorly grounded. Inspect the area around the ride and refrain from use if you see any frayed wires, if there are any standing pools of water near it, or if it is raining.

DINING OUT WITH YOUR CHILD

Mealtimes can be difficult enough at home with small children, never mind in a restaurant. But a restaurant can be a wonderful teaching ground for your children. It is a social environment that offers a colorful view of the big world outside of home. And besides, you cannot wait until he goes off to college to eat out again.

Choose your restaurants wisely. Opt for the family-oriented variety where a dropped glass of milk will not throw management into a frenzy. The telltale sign of the bad choice is a restaurant that does not have high chairs or booster seats. There is no welcome mat for your business at a restaurant that does not consider the needs of parents.

Prepare yourself before you even go. As in all other away from home situations, if you anticipate disaster you can greatly reduce its incidence. Step between your child and accidents.

☐ Pack a restaurant survival kit that includes:

- child-sized utensils
- a small plastic cup with a lid, or a bottle
- age-appropriate toys

- a coloring book and crayons; books
- a high-chair safety strap. This can be used in absence of a high chair for children who can sit well on their own. It can be wrapped around the adult chair to secure a toddler in place. If you are unsure, call ahead to the restaurant and ask if they have high chairs available.
- a bib and wipes

☐ Be careful of hot plates. You may want to ask your waiter or waitress to take back your order and change plates if they are unacceptably hot.

☐ Ask that your children be served first and as quickly as possible. Bring along or ask for some crackers if you know the wait may be a long one.

☐ With infants, try to feed them shortly before you leave, to avoid having to nurse or deal with bottle warming once at the restaurant.

☐ Remember, no honey for children under one.

☐ Remember that well-stocked diaper bag. Never leave home without it!

ELEVATOR SAFETY

Apartment living may necessitate the daily use of elevators. If your child is permitted to ride the elevator alone, make sure he knows:

☐ the elevator doors are not to be played with, pried open, or blocked from functioning normally

☐ how to locate and operate the alarm button and/or the emergency telephone should the elevator experience mechanical failure

☐ which floor he lives on and which button to push to stop there

☐ that the elevator is not an amusement but a mode of transportation

Safety requires thinking ahead and being prepared. By acting now and using common sense, you can reduce the stress of traveling with children and enjoy the adventure.

Chapter Eleven
Holiday Safety Check

Holidays can bring a young family to its knees! All of the excitement, change in routine, traveling, and special holiday events can spell stress for everyone. As a result, holidays have become prime time for accidents, especially Christmas, the Fourth of July, and Halloween.

As you gain the wisdom of parenthood you will become tuned to the events that can ruin the holiday spirit. Remind yourself before each holiday season to be especially sensitive to the following cues.

● *When your child is seeking attention:* Zero in on this cry for help. Stress is beginning to take its toll. Stop everything for a big hug and some special moments together. This time-out will help everyone relax and, we hope, head off potential problems.

● *When your child is getting less supervision:* It is not uncommon to visit the grandparents, kick up your feet, and expect everyone else to help out with the kids! Unfortunately, grandparents have their limits too, and are not as aware of your child's special needs. This opens the door for accidents. Make careful supervision a primary concern when you have guests over for dinner, visit relatives, or attend special family-oriented holiday events.

● *When children are tired and hungry:* Prepare yourself with a snack and juice tucked away for the inevitable growling tummy. Keep time changes in mind when you travel and hold your expectations to a minimum.

Fire and automobile accidents rate high on the list of holiday tragedy. Knowing this can help us concentrate on common-sense prevention throughout each season. The following checklists will alert you to the most obvious hazards.

NEW YEAR'S EVE

Alcohol is deadly! Keep this in mind while stocking the shelves for the midnight celebration. Alcohol should be kept well out of your child's reach.

EASTER

Avoid eating the hard-boiled eggs that are picked up at public hunts. Make sure homemade hard-boiled eggs are kept refrigerated before and after the Easter event.

MEMORIAL DAY

Family camping and crowded freeways set the stage for high accident statistics. Keep plans simple and check local activities before planning an involved vacation itinerary.

FOURTH OF JULY

Never permit children under the age of six to have fireworks. This includes sparklers and caps. Your best bet is to enjoy the public fireworks display and steer away from backyard extravaganzas.

LABOR DAY

Like Memorial Day, this is a good time to stay close to home during your child's early years. Remember, no small child is "water safe" even if swim lessons were successful this summer. Do not let your guard down around the pool!

HALLOWEEN

☐ Try to make do with the local recreation department's Halloween party.

☐ Trick-or-treat only at the homes of friends and neighbors you know. Enjoy being the chaperone!

☐ Choose or make Halloween costumes that are:

- fire retardant (heavy materials, no frilly or lightweight fabrics)
- easily visible at night. (Add reflector tape.)
- short in length and a proper fit
- maskless. Use nontoxic makeup instead of masks. (Check the ingredients label on cheap Halloween makeup kits, avoiding the toxic ingredient ferrocyanide.)

☐ Run candy bags through a volunteer hospital X-ray inspection.

☐ Discard treats with open wrappers.

☐ Keep homemade food and fruit only if you are certain who it came from. Notify police of any suspicious treats.

☐ Consider throwing your own neighborhood Halloween party.

☐ If you prefer to give nonedible treats, choose safe items that pose no choking threat to small children.

THANKSGIVING

Proper food preparation and storage is crucial to keeping the family healthy throughout the holiday weekend. Make sure your turkey is cooked to the correct temperature and perishable goodies are kept refrigerated until they are ready to be eaten. Don't neglect to refrigerate leftovers properly.

CHRISTMAS

☐ If you purchase a natural tree, make sure it is fresh! Some tips about choosing and caring for your tree:

- Try cutting it down yourself.
- Test needles: fresh needles bend between fingers without breaking.
- Keep it outside until you are ready to decorate.
- Cut the butt end diagonally a couple of inches above the original cut and keep the tree in water. Maintain the water level in the tree stand.
- Set up the tree clear of any heat source.
- Dispose of the tree when a lot of the needles begin to drop off.

☐ Avoid metal trees for the five-and-under age group. Sharp edges and the potential electrocution hazards pose a high risk.

☐ Artificial trees are not necessarily fire-resistant! Check the packaging and keep the trees away from any heat source.

☐ Break tradition if you must for a few years. Set the tree up with small children in mind. Try a small tree on a table or gate-off the tree area. Some families choose to live without a tree for a few years. Promise yourself you will give it some thought.

☐ Check tree lights every year! Check for frayed wire and empty, broken, or cracked sockets before plugging in. Give the lights a trial run for fifteen minutes. If they pass your observational test, put them on the tree.

☐ Always remember to turn the lights off before you leave the house.

☐ Never use indoor lights outdoors or the other way around.

☐ Once the lights are on the tree, add another step to your tradition. Trim away any needles or twigs from the light sockets. No light bulb should come in contact with the tree (make sure the lights are not plugged in when you are doing this).

☐ Do not overload extension cords or turn lights off by unplugging the extension and leaving it "live."

☐ Trimmings should be noncombustible or flame-resistant.

☐ Keep poisonous plants in mind. Mistletoe and holly are on the toxic plant list found in Appendix 1.

☐ Tinsel should be lead-free.

☐ Avoid incinerating Christmas wrapping paper in the fireplace.

☐ Save the strung popcorn projects for the older kids.

☐ Avoid glass ornaments. Choose stuffed ornaments with no small, detachable parts. Place ornaments out of your small child's reach.

BIRTHDAYS

At-home parties for preschoolers are the safest and easiest choice. Bring in entertainment if you want to splurge. Clowns, magicians, puppeteers and more are available through the Yellow Pages or local newspapers.

☐ Keep the menu simple and make sure all children stay seated while eating.

☐ Make sure you have a helper. It will make the entire event manageable.

☐ Hold the party activities in a childproofed room.

☐ Pick up any balloons that have popped.

☐ No tacks on Pin the Tail on the Donkey game; use tape.

☐ If you want parents to leave, you should inform them ahead of time. Parents of small children usually prefer to stay and monitor them.

☐ If you choose to venture out with a small group of children:

- Obtain advance permission from all parents.
- Inform parents of details including location, phone number, transportation arrangements, appropriate clothing, and time schedule.
- Line up help in advance.
- Inspect the birthday facilities ahead of time (know where the bathrooms are . . .)
- Take along the first-aid kit and have it handy in a childproof area of your car.
- Arrange for car seats ahead of time.
- Have a list of each child's home phone number or numbers where parents can be reached.
- Consider outings to nature centers, playgrounds,

pizza theaters, the zoo, circus or kids' theater, or a train ride.

☐ A word about party favors. Choose safe gifts that are all the same. Stickers, crayons, coloring books, or small books are appropriate. Avoid packaged, plastic party favors that appear breakable, sharp, and pointed or are small enough to pose a choking hazard.

If we have learned anything from our own holiday experiences, it is the importance of keeping the "holiday hype" under control. Try not to plant the seed of excitement too far in advance. Children will pick up on it without any words from you. This is especially hard at Christmas, but start small. Do not mention the Christmas party and the visit with Santa until you are dressing them to go. Do not bother with a November Christmas tree. And, by all means, try and keep your routine.

Chapter Twelve
Child Abuse

Child abuse is a sensitive topic, but one that must be addressed in a discussion of child safety. The question in every parent's mind is, "How can I prevent this from happening to my child?" The best way, again, is to arm yourself with information. Learn to recognize possible abuse. Teach your children in a loving, nonthreatening way about their rights as individuals and what constitutes a violation of that privacy.

The exploitation of children knows very few boundaries. Abusers can be friends, neighbors, relatives, doctors, even parents. Children are targeted for any number of reasons; they may seem vulnerable or needy somehow. They may be perceived as "special" or out of the ordinary. Whatever the reason, whoever the abuser, a child's physical and emotional well-being come under threat. Protect your children by teaching them. The following lists will help you and your child with that task.

INFORMATION YOUR CHILD SHOULD KNOW

☐ His full name, full address (including city and zip code), and telephone number including area code.

☐ A second telephone number. It could be the business number, your spouse's, or the number of a close relative or neighbor.

☐ Basic information about any medical condition such as allergies, asthma, etc.

☐ That you will never send anyone unfamiliar to pick him up from school or anywhere else. Teach him a code word to be used by anyone other than a parent who may be sent to pick him up.

☐ Never to play in vacant lots or abandoned buildings.

☐ Policemen and firemen are friends and can help him if he needs it.

☐ In any emergency he can dial O and speak to an operator who can offer assistance.

☐ If he becomes separated from you in a store, he should never leave that store. He should go to the nearest cash register, ask someone with a name tag if they work in the store, then ask for help.

☐ Repeat the following information periodically until it becomes automatic:

- Never accept a ride from a stranger.
- You have rights as an individual.
- Say "no" when an adult says something or touches you in a way that makes you uncomfortable. Tell your child that it is not appropriate for an adult to touch him on any part of his body that would be covered by a bathing suit.
- Do not be afraid to tell your mother or father if something like that does happen.

As a parent you must be prepared to try several approaches when discussing the issues with your children. Above all, remain calm and reassuring. Try to avoid voicing any specific consequences of being abducted or molested. When your child learns the information you wish him to have, praise him. Practice the safety lessons and repeat the information periodically.

PROTECTING YOUR CHILD FROM ABUSE AND KIDNAPPING

To complete the protective measures, it is important for parents to have information at their disposal as well. Here is a checklist:

☐ Keep recent photographs of your child on hand. Try to take a new one every six months. Avoid busy backgrounds. Clear views of the face are best.

☐ Keep an accurate description of your child including height, weight, identifying marks, hair/eye color, and any specific medical information such as allergies. In many metropolitan areas, microdots with this information can be affixed to your child's teeth.

☐ Make sure you know where to locate all medical and dental records. Find out how long the records are maintained. You may need to obtain copies before they are discarded.

☐ Have your child fingerprinted on a periodic basis. Your local sheriff's office may provide the service free of charge.

☐ You may wish to videotape your child, so as to provide a more complete visual record.

☐ Make sure you know the names of your child's friends and how you can reach them if you need to.

Scores of children are stolen every year—not by strangers, but by an estranged parent. If you find yourself in this potentially volatile situation, consider the following:

☐ If you suspect your spouse might try to abduct your child, you should obtain legal custody, either permanent or temporary. If custody has not been decided, there is no legal recourse if an abduction takes place.

☐ After being granted custody, obtain a passport for your child and inform the passport office that your child should not be allowed out of the country without written permission.

☐ If your spouse (or ex-) makes a threat to abduct, try and have witnesses present or tape-record the threat.

☐ Work out the terms of visitation to prevent possible abduction.

☐ Have all your spouse's vital information: social security number, driver's license number, credit information, and a list of relatives and friends.

☐ Try to maintain a civil if not friendly relationship with your ex-spouse for the sake of your child.

☐ Make sure your child's school, day-care center or baby-sitter has a certified copy of your custody order with a photograph of the noncustodial parent. Make sure the personnel of these facilities are fully aware of who is allowed to pick up the child, and who is not.

☐ Let your child know how he can look for you if you are ever separated. Make sure he knows your full name, address, and telephone number. Teach him how to make local and long-distance phone calls. Let him practice when you make calls of your own.

RECOGNIZING THE SIGNS OF ABUSE

If by some sad and unfortunate circumstance these attempts at protecting your child do not work, how will you know? What should you be looking for? How do you recognize signs of abuse?

From the behavioral aspect:

☐ Look for obvious changes in behavior: hesitancy to be around a particular adult, especially one who may have been a part of everyday life, and a reluctance to talk about the day's events.

☐ Exaggerated obedience.

☐ Aggressive behavior where none existed before.

☐ Hints at sexual activity or acting out sexual behavior with himself or his peers.

☐ Acting out roles that are not age-appropriate.

☐ Verbalization of detailed sexual behavior beyond his years. In other words, discussing acts or using words he would have no way of understanding.

☐ Diminished trust of specific adults.

☐ Antisocial behavior with peers; lack of concentration or diminished performance in school.

☐ Obvious sleep problems/nightmares.

☐ Withdrawal.

From the physical aspect:

☐ Any irregularities in the child's genital area, such as bruising, bleeding, swelling, or discharge.

☐ Complaints of pain or itching.

☐ Painful or difficult urination.

IF YOUR CHILD IS THE VICTIM OF ABUSE

☐ Discuss it as calmly as possible with your child.

☐ Have your child examined by a trusted pediatrician or one recommended by the authorities.

☐ Report the incident immediately to the police, taking care that the child does not have to repeat the story too often.

☐ Promptly arrange for counseling, not only for the child but for the entire family. Such an incident requires definite coping skills on everyone's part. A professional can be enormously helpful.

☐ Instruct your child to let you know immediately if the molester makes another attempt.

☐ Answer your child's questions or concerns with calm and understanding. Let him know that he is loved and that the incident was not his fault.

☐ Try to maintain a normal routine at home.

☐ Siblings should be informed that something has happened to their brother/sister but that he/she will be fine. A family counselor will help you with the best way of explaining the incident to siblings.

RECOGNIZE WHEN YOU NEED HELP

Part of your responsibility as a prepared parent is understanding when your stress level and your coping mechanism could directly affect the safety of your child.

Every parent experiences frustration when his child is disobedient. Every parent knows the feeling of being pushed to his or her limit. But how far does that limit extend and what should you do when you have reached it? The answers to these questions are with you. When and how you discipline your child have deep and lasting effects.

Learn to recognize when you need help. When your feelings become so intense that you want to act on them either verbally or physically on a regular basis, ask yourself these questions:

☐ Do you feel inadequate as a parent, overwhelmed by the task?

☐ Do you feel alone with nowhere to turn?

☐ Do you allow the little day-to-day problems of life and parenting to affect your thoughts and actions intensely?

☐ Have you ever harmed your child while feeling anger toward yourself?

☐ Do you look back to your own childhood and see signs of abuse or feel that you were mistreated?

☐ Do you ever experience confusing sexual feelings toward your own children?

☐ Have you ever acted on those feelings, or felt a strong urge to act on them?

If you answer yes to any of the above, remember you are not alone. There is help for you. Do not sit back and think these feelings will dissipate on their own. They are to be taken seriously as a possible threat to your child's safety. There is nothing more disconcerting than the feeling you are losing control, especially when it involves the little one you brought into this world. Here's what to do when you cannot cope:

☐ Organize your own support group. Talk to the other parents you know and suggest getting together on a regular basis to discuss the many stresses involved with parenting today. Time spent comparing notes about your child's behavior and ways of coping with it can be a positive way of expending the negative energy that comes from day-to-day stress. It is better for you, better for your child.

☐ Have a reciprocal arrangement with another mother or father so that if you need a break you can call and get some time for yourself outside the house and away from the kids, knowing you have reliable care.

☐ Call your local hotline. Many communities now have hotlines you can call when you have reached the crisis point or just need a sympathetic ear. The counselors are trained to answer your questions and concerns, suggest alternatives, and provide information. And do not worry. All calls are confidential and your identity will be protected.

☐ If you need somewhere else to turn, consider your local mental health center, family service agency, or physician.

☐ Contact Parents Anonymous, a crisis intervention program, at (800) 421-0353. In Illinois call (312) 663-3520.

BEFORE YOU DISCIPLINE YOUR CHILD

The following are a few suggestions to consider before resorting to the more traditional methods of discipline.

☐ Ensure that your child is fully aware of your values, your household rules, expected behavior, and the consequences of straying from what you deem acceptable.

☐ Become knowledgeable about child development. It will help you immensely in trying to understand why your child does what he does and when you can expect behavioral problems.

☐ Learn to recognize when your emotional level is rising to a potentially dangerous point and keep from disciplining your child until you have relaxed somewhat. An angry parent is far more likely to use physical tactics.

☐ Make sure you know exactly what happened in a situation you feel may require discipline. Allow the child to give his side of the story and avail yourself of all the information regarding the incident. It serves no positive purpose to punish an innocent child.

☐ Discuss your child's behavior with another person who can be objective. Verbalizing your tension and getting another person's opinion can help you be a more fair and understanding parent.

Appendix 1
Poisonous and Nonpoisonous Plants

Many common indoor and outdoor plants are poisons when chewed, swallowed, or rubbed on the skin. As with all toxins, the severity of the reaction depends on many factors including the quantity of poison and the child's height, weight, and age. Reactions may range from a mild skin rash or stomach cramp to severe complications including convulsions and coma. Take some simple precautions:

● Label indoor and outdoor plants with the correct botanical names. If necessary, take a piece of each plant with you to a plant store or nursery for positive identification.

● Put poison stickers on poisonous indoor plants, and place them well out of reach of curious children.

● Supervise children closely when they are playing outdoors near poisonous plants. Your knowledge of the plants in the garden is half the battle.

● Call your poison center immediately if you suspect that your child has put any part of a poisonous plant into her mouth.

The following list of poisonous plants is *not* all-inclusive. Call your poison center if you have any questions about possibly poisonous plants.

POISONOUS PLANTS

Angel's Trumpet *(Datura suaveolens)*
Azalea *(Rhododendron)*
Bird-of-Paradise *(Strelitzia reginae)*
Black Nightshade *(Solanum nigrum)*
Buttercup *(Ranunculus)*
Caladium *(Caladium)*
Castor Bean *(Ricinus communis)*
Chokecherry *(Prunus virginiana)*
Christmas Pepper *(Capsicum annuum)*
Climbing Nightshade *(Solanum dulcamara)*
Daffodil *(Narcissus)*
Daphne *(Daphne Mezereum)*
Deadly Nightshade *(Atropa Belladonna)*
Delphinium *(Delphinium)*
Dumb Cane *(Dieffenbachia)*
Elephant's-Ear *(Colocasia esculenta)*
English Ivy *(Hedera Helix)*
Foxglove *(Digitalis purpurea)*
Fruit pits: apple, peach, apricot, wild cherry,
pear, plum
Holly *(Ilex)*
Hyacinth *(Hyacinthus orientalis)*
Hydrangea *(Hydrangea)*
Iris *(Iris)*
Jack-in-the-Pulpit *(Arisaema triphyllum)*
Jerusalem Cherry *(Solanum pseudocapsicum)*
Jimsonweed *(Datura Stramonium)*
Jonquil *(Narcissus Jonquilla)*
Lantana *(Lantana)*
Lily-of-the-Valley *(Convallaria majalis)*
Mayapple *(Podophyllum peltatum)*

Mistletoe *(Viscum album)*
Morning-Glory *(Ipomoea Learii)*
Mountain Laurel *(Kalmia latifolia)*
Narcissus *(Narcissus)*
Oleander *(Nerium oleander)*
Philodendron *(Philodendron)*
Pokeweed *(Phytolacca americana)*
Pothos *(Scindapsus aureus, Raphidophora aurea)*
Privet *(Ligustrum vulgare)*
Rhododendron *(Rhododendron)*
Rhubarb leaves *(Rheum officinale)*
Sweet Pea *(Lathyrus odoratus)*
Swiss-cheese plant *(Monstera deliciosa)*
Tomato leaves *(Lycopersicon esculentum)*
Yew *(Taxus)*
Virginia Creeper *(Parthenocissus quinquefolia)*
Wisteria *(Wisteria)*

NONPOISONOUS PLANTS

Take the following list with you on your plant-shopping trip. It will help you make the right choices for a childproofed home.

African violet *(Saintpaulia ionantha)*
Begonia *(Begonia)*
Christmas Cactus *(Schlumbergera Bridgesii, Zygocactus truncactus)*
Coleus *(Coleus Blumei)*
Dandelion *(Taraxacum officinale)*
Dracaena *(Dracaena)*
Impatiens *(Impatiens)*
Jade *(Crassula argentea)*
Marigold *(Tagetes)*
Peperomia *(Peperomia caperata)*

Poinsettia *(Euphorbia pulcherrima)*
Prayer Plant *(Maranta)*
Purple Passion *(Gynura aurantiaca)*
Rose *(Rosa)*
Schefflera *(Brassaia actinophylla)*
Snake Plant *(Sansevieria trifasciata)*
Spider *(Chlorophytum comosum)*
Swedish Ivy *(Plectranthus australia)*
Wandering Jew *(Tradescantia fluminensis)*
Wax Plant *(Hoya carnosa)*
Wild Strawberry *(Fragaria)*
Zebra Plant *(Aphelandra squarrosa)*

Appendix 2
Toxic Substances

A poison is any food, chemical, plant, liquid that is used improperly or in improper amounts. Anything used in a way that it was not intended. Think about it like this: if the "wild one" swallows a prune pit, consider it a poison and call your poison control center for help. That goes for bites and stings too.

When in doubt or even slightly concerned, call immediately. Never attempt to treat a poison emergency at home before contacting a poison control center. There is only one exception to this rule: you should act on your own when a toxin gets on the skin or in the eyes. In these cases, flush with running water immediately for at least fifteen minutes. Then call your center.

Teach your children that the following products are unsafe. Children learn by example. It is a parent's responsibility to keep these products out of reach and display caution while using them. Use poison stickers as a teaching tool by placing them on toxins around the home and explaining in simple terms that the sticker signifies "danger." Poison stickers can be obtained:

- free by sending a self-addressed, stamped, business-size envelope to your poison control center
- by calling the regional poison control center nearest you and requesting their poison prevention materials

- by sending $1 to the Institute of Education Communications, Children's Hospital of Pittsburgh, 125 DeSoto Street, Pittsburgh, PA 15213.

Have syrup of ipecac on hand for an emergency but *never* use it to treat a poisoning without first contacting your poison center and following their instructions. Activated charcoal is another poison antidote. In most cases, this product is hard to find in stores for two reasons: it's difficult to administer, and often a victim can be transported to a hospital and treated within a reasonable period of time without it. Product research is currently being conducted to develop a more practical form of activated charcoal to use in emergency situations. Today, most victims could arrive at the hospital before the antidote takes effect and valuable time may be wasted. If you live in an area that is not near a hospital you might consider keeping this product on hand. It is also a good idea to have it in the first-aid kit for the camping trip or mountain cabin.

LIST OF TOXIC SUBSTANCES

BATHROOM

soaps and shampoos
detergents and cleansers
deodorizers
suntan lotions
medicines of all kinds including:
- vitamins
- prescription drugs
- over-the-counter drugs
- herbal/folk/home remedies

- veterinary
- illegal

cosmetics, especially alcohol-containing cosmetics such as:
  - perfume
  - cologne
  - aftershave
  - mouthwash

deodorants
toilet-bowl cleaners*

BEDROOM

medicines*
cosmetics
nail polish and remover
detergents and cleansers

KITCHEN

vitamins
drain cleaners
furniture polish
pet medicines
electric dishwasher detergents*
oven cleaners*
ammonia
detergents and bleach
disinfectants
metal cleaners
rat poison and insecticides*

* Indicates the toxins most commonly involved in poison emergencies.

GARAGE

lime and fertilizers
paint and varnishes
turpentine, kerosene, solvents
gasoline
antifreeze
weed killers
insecticides*

STORAGE AREAS

mothballs
rat and insect poison*

AROUND THE HOME

cigarettes, cigars, and butts
felt-tip markers
flaking paint
insulation
plants
alcoholic beverages*

* Indicates the toxins most commonly involved in poison emergencies.

Appendix 3
Regional Poison Control Centers

Two distinct studies concluded that more accurate information is provided for a poisoning emergency when a regional poison center hotline is called rather than a local poison center. Regional centers staff highly trained and nationally certified poison information specialists who can answer your questions with the most up-to-date reference materials at their fingertips. The following list of regional centers is presented as a resource. Check the list for one in your area and call for their information packet. Keep the hotline number of this center handy in case of a poison emergency.

ALABAMA

Alabama Poison Center
809 University Blvd. East
Tuscaloosa, AL 35401
(205) 345-0600 (Admin.); (800) 462-0800
(AL only)

ARIZONA

Arizona Poison Control System
Arizona Health Sciences Center, Rm. 3204K
University of Arizona
Tucson, AZ 85724
(602) 626-7899 (Admin.); (602) 626-6016 (Tucson)

(602) 253-3334 (Phoenix); (800) 362-0101
(AZ only)

CALIFORNIA

Los Angeles County Medical Association Regional
Poison Control Center
1925 Wilshire Blvd.
Los Angeles, CA 90057
(213) 664-2121 (Admin.); (213) 484-5151

UCDMC Regional Poison Control Center
2315 Stockton Blvd.
Sacramento, CA 95817
(916) 453-3414 (Admin.); (916) 453-3692

San Diego Regional Poison Center
UCSD Medical Center
225 Dickson St.
San Diego, CA 92103
(619) 294-3666

San Francisco Bay Area Regional Poison Control
Center
San Francisco General Hospital, Room 1E86
1001 Potrero Ave.
San Francisco, CA 94110
(415) 821-8324 (Admin); (415) 476-6600

COLORADO

Rocky Mountain Poison Center
645 Bannock St.
Denver, CO 80204-4507
(303) 893-7774 (Admin); (303) 629-1123
(800) 332-3073 (CO only)
(800) 525-5042 (MT only)
(800) 442-2702 (WY only)

FLORIDA

Tampa Bay Regional Poison Control Center
P.O. Box 18582
Tampa, FL 33679

(813) 251-6911 (Admin); (813) 253-4444;
(800) 282-3171

GEORGIA

Georgia Poison Control Center
Box 26066, 80 Butler St., SE
Atlanta, GA 30335

INDIANA

Indiana Poison Center
Wishard Memorial Hospital
1001 W. Tenth St.
Indianapolis, IN 46202
(317) 630-6382 (Admin); (317) 630-7351;
(800) 382-9097; (317) 630-6666 (TTY)

KENTUCKY

Kentucky Regional Poison Control Center
    of Kosair Children's Hospital
P.O. Box 35070
Louisville, KY 40232-5070
(502) 562-7264 (Admin); (502) 589-8222;
(800) 722-5725 (KY only)

LOUISIANA

Louisiana Regional Poison Control Center
Louisiana State University School of Medicine in
    Shreveport
P.O. Box 33932
Shreveport, LA 71130-3932
(318) 673-6364 (Admin); (318) 425-1524;
(800) 535-0525

MARYLAND

Maryland Poison Center
23 N. Pine St.
Baltimore, MD 21201
(301) 528-7604 (Admin); (301) 528-7701;
(800) 492-2414 (MD only)

MASSACHUSETTS

Massachusetts Poison Control System
300 Longwood Ave.
Boston, MA 02115
(617) 735-6607 (Admin); (617) 232-2120;
(800) 682-9211

MICHIGAN

Blodgett Regional Poison Center
1840 Wealthy, SE
Grand Rapids, MI 49506
(616) 774-7854 (Admin); (800) 442-4571
    (AC 616 only);
(800) 632-2727 (MI only)

Poison Control Center
Children's Hospital of Michigan
3901 Beaubien Blvd.
Detroit, MI 48201
(313) 745-5329 (Admin); (313) 745-5711;
(800) 462-6642 (AC313 only); (800) 572-1655

MINNESOTA

Hennepin Regional Poison Center
Hennepin County Medical Center
701 Park Ave.
Minneapolis, MN 55415
(612) 347-3144 (Admin); (612) 347-3141;
(612) 347-6219 (TTY)

Minnesota Regional Poison Center
St. Paul Ramsey Medical Center
640 Jackson St.
St. Paul, MN 55101
(612) 221-3096 (Admin); (612) 221-2113;
(800) 222-1222

MISSOURI

Cardinal Glennon Children's Hospital,
    Regional Poison Center

1465 S. Grand Blvd.
St. Louis, MO 63104
(314) 772-8300 (Admin); (314) 772-5200;
(800) 392-9111 (MO only)

NEW JERSEY

New Jersey Poison Information and Education
  System
201 Lyons Ave.
Newark, NJ 07112
(201) 926-7443 (Admin); (201) 923-0764
(800) 962-1253 (NJ only)

NEW MEXICO

New Mexico Poison and Drug Information Center
University of New Mexico
Albuquerque, NM 87131
(505) 277-4261 (Admin); (505) 843-2551;
(800) 432-6866 (NM only)

NEBRASKA

Mid Plains Poison Center
8301 Dodge St.
Omaha, NE 68114
(402) 390-5434 (Admin); (402) 390-5400;
(800) 642-9999 (NE only);
(800) 228-9515 (surrounding states)

NEW YORK

Long Island Regional Poison Control Center
Nassau County Medical Center
2201 Hempstead Turnpike
East Meadow, NY 11554
(516) 542-3707 (Admin); (516) 542-2323

New York City Poison Control Center
455 1st Ave., Rm. 123
New York, NY 10016
(212) 340-4497 (Admin); (212) 340-4494;
(800) 225-0658 (Outside NY only)

NORTH CAROLINA

Duke University Poison Control Center
Box 3007
Duke University Medical Center
Durham, NC 27710
(919) 684-4438 (Admin); (919) 684-8111;
(800) 672-1697 (NC only)

OHIO

Central Ohio Poison Center
Columbus Children's Hospital
700 Children's Drive
Columbus, OH 43205
(614) 461-2012 (Admin); (614) 228-1323;
(800) 682-7625

Southwest Regional Poison Control System
c/o Drug & Poison Information Center
231 Bethesda Ave. M.L. #144
Cincinnati, OH 45267-0144
(513) 872-5111; (800) 872-5111

PENNSYLVANIA

Pittsburgh Poison Center
3705 5th Ave. at DeSoto St.
Pittsburgh, PA 15213
(412) 647-5600; (412) 681-6669

RHODE ISLAND

Rhode Island Poison Center
Rhode Island Hospital
593 Eddy St.
Providence, RI 02902
(401) 277-5906 (Admin); (401) 277-5727;
(401) 277-8062 (TTY)

TEXAS

North Central Texas Poison Center
P.O. Box 35926
Dallas, TX 75235

(214) 920-2586 (Admin); (214) 920-2400;
(800) 441-0040 (TX only)

Texas State Poison Center
University of Texas Medical Branch
Galveston, TX 77550-2780
(409) 761-3332 (Admin); (409) 765-1420;
(713) 654-1701 (Houston)
(516) 478-4490 (Austin); (800) 392-8548 (TX only)

UTAH

Intermountain Regional Poison Control Center
50 N. Medical Dr., Bldg. 428
Salt Lake City, UT 84132
(801) 581-7504 (Admin); (801) 581-2151;
(800) 662-0062 (UT only)

WEST VIRGINIA

West Virginia Poison Center
West Virginia University School of Pharmacy
3110 McCorckle Ave., SE
Charleston, WV 25304
(304) 347-1212 (Admin); (304) 348-4211;
(800) 642-3625 (WV only)

WASHINGTON, D.C.

National Capital Poison Center
Georgetown University Hospital
3800 Reservoir Rd., NW
Washington, D.C. 20007
(202) 625-6073 (Admin); (202) 625-3333

Appendix 4
Resources

CORPORATE PUBLICATIONS ON CHILD SAFETY

The following publications are provided free upon request:

Publication:

"Keeping Danger Out of Reach"

> Aetna Life & Casualty
> Film Librarian, PR & Advertising Dept.
> 151 Farmington Avenue
> Hartford, CT 06115

Publications:

"A Handbook of Child Safety"
"Guidelines—Child Safety"

> Gerber Products Co.
> 445 State Street
> Fremont, MI 49412
> Attn: Medical Marketing Service

Publications:

"Guide for the First Time Babysitter"
"Parenting Insights"
"Baby Care Basics"
"How Your Baby Grows"

"Fire Safety"
"First Aid for the Family"
"Planning for Safety"
"Child Safety"
"Health & Safety Educational Materials Catalogue"

> Metropolitan Life Insurance Co.
> 1 Madison Ave.
> New York, NY 10010

Publication:
"Child Lures: A Guide to Prevent Abduction"

> Ralston Purina Co.
> St. Louis, MO 63164

Publications:
"Learning About Labels"
"The ABC's of Toys and Play"

> Toy Manufacturers of America
> P.O. Box 866
> Madison Square Station
> New York, NY 10159

CHILD ABUSE

For information regarding child abuse, contact:

> National Center on Abuse and Neglect
> U.S. Dept. of Health & Human Services
> P.O. Box 1182
> Washington, D.C. 20013
> (202) 245-2856

> National Committee for the Prevention of Child
> Abuse
> 332 S. Michigan Ave., Suite 1250
> Chicago, IL 60604

National Center for Missing & Exploited Children
1835 K Street, Suite 700
Washington, D.C. 20004
(202) 634-9821

RECOMMENDED READING

Parental Child Stealing
Michael W. Agopian

> Lexington Books
> 125 Spring St.
> Lexington, MA 02173

Child Abuse & Neglect
H. Giaretto

> Ballinger Publications
> 54 Church St.
> Harvard Square
> Cambridge, MA 02138

*Private Zone: A Book Teaching Children Sexual Assault
Prevention Tools*
Frances S. Dayee

> The Charles Franklin Press
> 7821 175th St. SW
> Edmonds, WA 98020

DAY CARE

To obtain information on choosing good day care for
your child contact:

> Child Care Action Campaign
> 99 Hudson St., Rm. 1233
> New York, NY 10013

National Association for the Education of Young
Children
1834 Connecticut Ave., NW
Washington, D.C. 20009
(202) 232-8777

U.S. GOVERNMENT AGENCIES

Consumer Product Safety Commission
Washington, D.C. 20207
(800) 492-CPSC Continental U.S.
(800) 492-8104 Maryland
(800) 638-8333 Hawaii, Alaska, Puerto Rico, and
the Virgin Islands

If you or your child have been injured by a consumer
product, call or write the CPSC. The hearing-impaired
may call (800) 638-8279.

Food & Drug Administration
5600 Fishers Lane, HFE 88
Rockville, MD 20857
(301) 443-3170

To obtain information about or report a hazardous food,
drug, cosmetic, or medical device, contact the FDA.

National Highway Traffic Safety Commission
400 Seventh St., SW
Washington, D.C. 20590
(800) 424-9393; (202) 426-9123

National Child Passenger Safety Administration
1705 DeSales St., NW, Suite 300
Washington, D.C. 20036

To obtain information on seat belts, child safety seats,
etc. contact the NHTSC or the NCPSA. To report de-
fects in such equipment, contact the NHTSC.

Consumer Federation of America
1424 16th St., SW, Suite 604
Washington, D.C. 20036
(202) 387-6121

This is the largest consumer group in the country.

National Fire Protection Agency
Battermarch Park
Quincy, MA 02269
(800) 344-3555

National Reye's Syndrome Foundation
426 N. Lewis
Bryan, OH 43506
(419) 636-2579

National Safety Council
444 N. Michigan Ave.
Chicago, IL 60611
(312) 527-4800

National Sudden Infant Death Syndrome
   Foundation
2 Metro Plaza, Suite 205
8240 Professional Place
Landover, MD 20785

Children's Defense Fund
122 C Street, NW
Washington, D.C. 20001

This organization provides information about issues such as homeless children, health care for poor children, and federal budget allocations for "children's issues."

National Center for Clinical Infant Programs
733 15th Street, NW, Suite 912
Washington, D.C. 20005

To obtain information regarding your child's mental health and development contact the NCCIP.

SAFETY CAMPAIGN RESOURCES

BURN SAFETY

"Stop, Drop and Roll"
Alisa Ann Buch
20944 Sherman Way, Suite 115
Canoga Park, CA 91303

Pamphlet— "Learn Not To Burn"

DISEASE CONTROL

"Teddy Wants You to Wash Your Hands" (Poster/Buttons)
National Cancer Institute (Pediatric Branch)
(301) 496-4256

EYE SAFETY

"Seymour Safely"
American Optometric Association
243 N. Lindbergh Blvd.
St. Louis, MO 63141

TOY SAFETY

World Against Toys Causing Harm (W.A.T.C.H.)
c/o Edward Swartz
The John and Ebenezer Hancock House
10 Marshall St.
Boston, MA 02108

SAFETY IN GENERAL

Channing L. Bele Co., Inc.
200 State Road
South Deerfield, MA 01373

This company produces a number of scriptographic booklets on health- and safety-related issues. Write for a current price list and catalogue.

Adam Walsh Child Resource Center
1876 N. University Dr., Suite 306
Fort Lauderdale, FL 33322

Teachers can obtain a Teacher's Packet ($30.00) entitled "The Adam Walsh Center Safety with Strangers Program."

SAFETY IN GENERAL

Channing L. Bete Co., Inc.
200 State Road
South Deerfield, MA 01373

This company produces a number of scriptographic booklets on health and safety related topics. Write for a current price list and catalogue.

Adam Walsh Child Resource Center
1876 N. University Dr., Suite 306
Fort Lauderdale, FL 33322

Features an optional a Teachers Packet ($20.00) entitled "The Adam Walsh Child Center Safety with Strangers Program."

Bibliography

Arena, M. D.; Jay M. and Miriam Bachar Settle. *Child Safety Is No Accident: A Guide to Safety Promotion and Accident Prevention.* New York: Berkley Books, 1987.

Baker, Eugene H. *Safety First.* Lake Forest: Creative Education, 1980.

Fontana, Vincent J. *A Parent's Guide to Child Safety.* New York: Crowell, 1973.

Gillis, Jack, and Mary E. Fise. *The Childwise Catalog.* New York: Pocket Books, 1986.

Harmon, Murl. *A New Vaccine for Child Safety.* Jenkintown, PA: Safety Now Co., 1976.

Kalt, Bryson R., and Ralph Bass. *The Mother's Guide to Child Safety.* New York: Grosset & Dunlap, 1971.

Rinzler, Carol Ann. *The Children's Medicine Chest.* New York: Berkley Books, 1984.

Swartz, Edward M. *Toys That Kill.* New York: Vintage Books, 1986.

Stewart, Arlene. *Childproofing Your Home.* Reading, MA: Addison-Wesley, 1984.

PAMPHLETS

"Parent's Guide," Adam Walsh Resource Center, Fort Lauderdale.

"It Shouldn't Hurt To Be A Child," The National Committee for the Prevention of Child Abuse, Chicago, 1986.

DEVICE COUNT LIST

The following list is intended to help you keep track of the devices you may wish to purchase after making a room-by-room tour of your home and yard.

electrical caps _____

electrical covers _____

doorknob covers _____

corner guards _____

foam/tape _____

edging material (number of feet) _____

latches _____

gates _____

smoke alarms _____

carpet tape _____

Miscellaneous items: _____

_____

_____

_____

Special Notes: _____

_____

_____

_____

_____

_____

MARY METZGER and CINTHYA P. WHITTAKER are the founders of KinderKraft, Inc., a company which provides child safety workshops, CPR instruction, and home consultations, and produces the Babyproofing Kit. They are also active lobbyists in the area of child safety and accident prevention. Both Metzger and Whittaker live in Arlington, Virginia.

MARY MURRAY and GINGER P. WHITAKER are the founders of Kindersafe, Inc., a company which provides child safety workshops, CPR instruction and home consultations and produce the babyproofing kit. They are also active lobbyists in the area of child safety and accident prevention. Both Murray and Whitaker live in Arlington, Virginia.